GREAT
PAPER
CRAFTS

GREAT PAPER CRAFTS

Ideas, Tips & Techniques

Judy Ritchie and Jamie Kilmartin

with *Deborah Cannarella*

HUGH LAUTER LEVIN ASSOCIATES, INC.

PROJECT DIRECTOR: LESLIE CONRON CAROLA
DESIGN: ELIZABETH JOHNSBOEN, JOHNSBOEN DESIGN
COPY EDITOR; DEBORAH TEIPEL ZINDELL
EDITORIAL PRODUCTION: MELISSA PAYNE

Projects are credited to designers on page; projects without
credit have been created by Judy Ritchie or Jamie Kilmartin.

Printed in Hong Kong.

Distributed by Publishers Group West

ACKNOWLEDGMENTS
Thank you to the participants from all across the country—
individual designers and manufacturers—for their generous
contributions to this project. Marilynne Oskamp from Ecstasy
Crafts; Andrea Grossman and Sheryl Kumli from Mrs.
Grossman's Paper Company; Kathy Yoshida from Hanko
Design; Sherry Crocker from Lake City Crafts; Nathalie
Métivier from Magenta; Cherryl Moote from Moote Points;
Amy Kennedy and Adrienne Kennedy from My Sentiments
Exactly!; JoAnn Ellis from Petite Motifs, Lara Zazzi and Cindi
Nelson from Savvy Stamps; Kacey Carey; Laurie Goodson;
Pam Klassen; Kim Smith; Trish Turay; Jan Williams.

CONTENTS

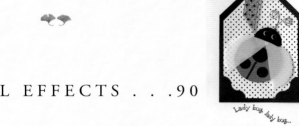

INTRODUCTION

········

Paper is a wonderful material—it's colorful, sensual, and easy to store and handle. And for the paper crafter, it's an infinitely versatile canvas. You can make note cards that friends will save forever, gift packages almost too lovely to open, and personalized stationery that is creatively and unmistakably yours. With just a few basic tools and techniques—as little as a single sheet of paper and a charming rubber stamp—you can create a varied array of effects and one-of-a-kind works of art.

Great Paper Crafts offers you more than 100 different ways to think about paper. The authors—and paper artists and designers from throughout the country—offer you a sampling of some of their favorite projects. You can follow the techniques step by step—or just let yourself be inspired to create completely innovative designs. Whether you are a beginner or an experienced paper crafter, this book will provide you with plenty of ideas, inspiration, and instruction. You'll learn how to fold, cut, stamp, tear, punch, pierce, emboss, stitch, and otherwise manipulate and embellish paper to create endless effects. Scrapbookers, too, will love this treasure trove of ideas for new ways to enhance their pages. We have even included a special chapter on altered books so you can showcase your paper craft techniques "between covers" in a lasting, original work of art.

Trish Turay

To get started, you really need only two simple tools—a little paper and a lot of creativity. Your designs can be as simple or complex as you want to make them. Each style has its own unique charm. Even a simple technique like punch art can yield so many different effects that no two projects will ever look the same.

Start with a technique that feels most comfortable to you. As you begin to experiment—and see the wonderful results—you'll feel the urge to try another, and then another new technique. You'll also discover several specialty techniques, such as paper weaving, embroidery, quilling, and spirelli, to add drama and interest to your paper creations. Eventually, you will have a wide array of techniques at your disposal—to mix and match in ways best suited to the special purpose, person, or project you have in mind.

Work with exotic specialty papers, like silkscreened Japanese *chiyogami,* or with assorted, favorite remnants left over from other projects. Or have some fun with decorative

Jan Williams

or handmade papers. Cut them into mats with fancy edgings, fold them into frames, or piece them to create a geometric mosaic. Add extra interest and dimension by embossing and piercing sheets of vellum, iris-folding or embroidering a central motif, weaving or quilting a background pattern—all described in these pages. Share sentimentality or silliness by adding delicate lace borders or whimsical charms. Accent the page with imaginatively cropped photographs, colorful stickers, and fanciful punched shapes. The possibilities are endless—and your choices will, like your own signature, make your projects unmistakably your own.

There are so many wonderful papers, in every color, pattern, texture, and weight imaginable. There are handmade papers, *washi* or rice papers, pastel pearlescents, smooth and patterned parchments, mulberry papers, crinkle papers, translucent vellums, metal foils, lace, and linen. But don't forget about the less exotic candidates that you already have on hand—tissue paper, sheet music, paper doilies, pages from books or magazines, greeting cards, junk mail, old newspapers, postcards, maps, cancelled stamps, ticket stubs, seed packets, soap wrappers, foreign currency. Even those scraps you might not otherwise look twice at may yield incredible effects when used in just the right way.

Choose papers that best suit the mood of the occasion or the theme of your design. For a children's birthday invitation, you might use cardstock in bright, primary colors. For a wedding invitation, you might use soft muted shades of velvet and vellum papers. But the most important rule is to choose papers that capture your eye and your imagination. Open your mind to every possibility—and your designs will be full of interest and character. One wonderful paper can become the springboard for your entire design!

Laurie Goodson

When you have chosen your paper, you'll need some basic tools. Some techniques may have their own specialty materials—stamps and punches, for example—but these few tools will help with every technique.

You'll need a craft knife with sharp blades and a metal straightedge ruler to make clean, straight cuts. You'll also need a padded surface—a gridded craft mat, self-healing mat, or a dense foam pad—for cutting, setting eyelets, or working with ponce, piercing, and embossing tools. Straightedge scissors, pinking shears, and embroidery and manicure scissors will come in handy, too. Keep a pair of fine-pointed tweezers nearby, for handling stickers and other small pieces and shapes. Make sure you have plenty of paints, crayons, pens, markers, and pencils in an array of colors.

You have your choice of adhesives. Polyvinyl acetate glue—white craft glue—works well for just about any type of job. Glue sticks dry more quickly so you'll have to work a little faster. Double-sided transparent tape is great for making envelopes, and you'll need foam-mounting tape, dots, and pads to pop stickers and other three-dimensional objects.

There are many specialty items available, too, but start simple. You can create wonderful paper craft projects for a very long time before you exhaust all the creative possibilities of these basic supplies.

Designing is a natural, intuitive process. Your own instincts will be your best guide—but as you begin to plan your project, consider these few basic design principles.

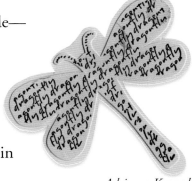

A successful design should have a strong focal point. A focal point is the area of the design that immediately draws the eye. It may be as simple as a stamped daisy smack dab in the middle of the note card. You can highlight your focal point for extra emphasis by adding a decorative accent—perhaps a purple sequin in the flower's center!

Adrienne Kennedy

A good design should also have variety of shape, color, and texture. Similar or compatible shapes, colors, and textures work together to create a harmonious effect. All the elements should support and enhance each other. Be careful not to introduce too many elements, however. You may lose the focal point and create a random, chaotic effect. When in doubt, keep it simple. It's sometimes easy to get carried away! As you're working—and before committing yourself with glue!—step back once in a while to see how the whole design is working together. Trust your eye.

Kim Smith

Great Paper Crafts is divided into the following sections, each one focusing on a different method used by paper crafters:

Rubber Stamping—Rubber stamping is one of the easiest ways to get started in paper craft. Stamp a design several times to create a decorative background—or stamp it once as the central motif. Stamping inks, in solid, metallic, and rainbow colors, allow you to vary the finished effects. Change the color of the ink, and you can create an entirely different effect. Accent the stamping with an extra detail—a ribbon, button, or charm—to add dimension and make the design uniquely your own.

Punch Art—Punches are small handheld paper cutters. But what they can do! With just a flick of your thumb, you can embellish edgings, borders, and overlays. You can even use the small punched-out "negative" shape as a stencil, embossing template, or die cut within the same design—or save it for later use. You can also work with negative shapes to build decorative sculptures. Think layers—and you'll discover a world of potential in that small punched shape.

Sticker Art—Stickers couldn't be easier. Just remove the backing and you're ready to go! Choose a shape or style that suits the theme of your project and place one or more to create a central motif or a decorative accent. To create depth, you can even position stickers to partially overlap the edge of your card or paper. You can also mount them on small foam-adhesive pads—rather than directly onto the paper—so that they "pop" away from the paper's surface.

Mrs. Grossman's Paper Company

Folding—Decorative folding instantly adds visual interest, texture, and dimension. The Japanese craft of origami and the Dutch techniques of tea bag folding and iris folding provide variations in method and design.

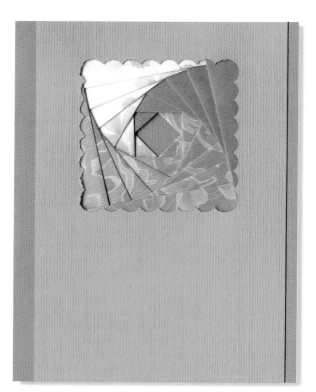

You can fold paper to create simple or complex mats, frames, envelopes, central motifs, or decorative details. The paper texture, weight, and color and pattern (on each side) determine the finished effect. But the key to any type of folding is the accuracy of your first fold. If your first fold is incorrect or badly aligned, the rest of your folds will be, too. Make sure each fold is clean and crisp—and don't be afraid to use a bone folder or your thumbnail to make sure it is.

Collage—Collage is a freeform art form—so the best way to begin is with a sense of freedom and fun. Let yourself play by selecting papers and objects that you like the look or feel of—then see where your eye and hand lead you. Trust yourself and follow your instincts. Allow yourself to explore every shape, texture, color, and material that appeals to you. Arrange and rearrange the elements and enjoy the process. Often, the best collage is one you could never have imagined when you began.

Special Effects—Paper crafters can easily borrow techniques from other arts and crafts. Like fabric, paper can be pieced, woven, and stitched—as in the techniques of paper quilting, weaving, and embroidery. Paper pieces can also be arranged like ceramic tiles, to create mosaic-like geometry pages. Spirelli, or string art, is a thread-wrapping technique that also produces a geometric effect. With quilling, or scroll work, paper crafters assemble pictures and designs with rolled strips of paper.

Altered Books—Gather old books from your shelves, rummage through garage sales, or borrow from friends. An old book provides paper crafters with hundreds of blank canvases! The art of altered books is a variation on the art of collage, and the same design principles apply. Combine elements, textures, and colors in a harmonious composition to create a single mood or theme—but also think about how the pages will work together as the viewer "reads" the book. Try combining techniques on a single "spread" of two pages—or create a book-length sampler of techniques by featuring a different paper craft on every spread.

Cherryl Moote

Jan Williams

Great Paper Crafts includes an illustrated glossary that defines many of the key terms used by paper crafters, and a source guide that tells you where to find the materials used for each project described in the book. We have also provided several templates that you may find helpful. So, get started, and have fun!

RUBBER STAMPING

Stamping is playful, simple, and fun. It's a great way to add a personal touch to gift packages, recipe cards, thank-you notes, and stationery or to add extra-special details to the pages of a scrapbook or an artistic altered book. There is such a wide range of effects you can create—and so many stamps to choose from—that you'll never run out of new things to try. And best of all, the technique itself is so easy, you can focus all of your attention on creating designs.

Stamping is a perfect way to decorate paper for every purpose and occasion. You can create the simplest designs—with just a single stamp—or combine stamping with one or several other paper craft techniques. Choose picture stamps that express the theme of your artwork—a Christmas wreath for a holiday package, bundles of balloons for a party invitation, a ballerina for your daughter's scrapbook page. Or choose dots, small hearts, or stars and stamp multiple repeats to create a border or background effect. You can even stamp letters of the alphabet—or complete words—to add a meaningful message. And the wide variety of stamping inks, in a range of solid, metallic, and rainbow colors, allows you to add even more variety to the finished effects.

Experiment with combining stamps and layering or overlapping them slightly to create different effects. Stamp on any type of paper—from brown paper bags to lovely vellums and parchments. And of course, the many colors and types of ink available allow you to create endless variations. Whoever thought it could be so easy to make something so charming?

SIMPLE STAMPING

*S*tamping, even at its simplest—a single stamp and only black ink—does not have to look simple at all. The trick is to start with colored paper, as with this cheerful birthday card. The centers and petals of the flowers and the leaves are colored with colored pencils. The pre-printed ribbon and the posy brads add just the right finishing touch.

Creating the Project

1. Stamp your design with black ink onto your colored paper.

2. Color areas and details of the image with colored pencils. You might want to pick up colors from your cardstock or ribbon or other embellishments.

3. Turn the scalloped square punch upside down. Insert the stamped paper and position the image where you want it. Punch out the square.

4. Mount the punched square onto the cardstock.

5. Fold a length of ribbon in half lengthwise and cut the unfolded ends on a diagonal to form the flag ends.

6. Lay the ribbon in place on the card. With a fine-tipped awl, pierce holes in either end of the ribbon through the cardstock to insert the brads. Open the brads on the inside of the card front.

TIP

To conceal the open prongs of the brads inside the note card, glue a sheet or strip of paper to the cardstock. Decorate the paper or add a special sentiment or message.

Stamping in a color other than black creates a soft subtle effect. In this card, even the message is stamped in blue ink.

PRETTY & SIMPLE

*T*his assortment of floral motifs was created by stamping with one color of ink and then coloring with several vibrant shades of colored pencils. The handful of violets and the multicolored bunch of flowers on this page are each made with a single stamp.

Creating the Project

1. To make the single posy card, stamp the vase onto the cardstock. Then stamp it again onto removable masking material.

2. Trim the mask at the top along the front rim of the mouth of the vase.

3. Lay the mask over the stamped image on the cardstock, being careful to align the rims of the vase.

4. Now stamp the flower so that the bottom of the stem overlaps the mask. Remove the mask—the stem will appear to be extending out of the vase.

5. Color the vase by blending two or more compatible shades.

Dave Brethauer

Dave Brethauer

The multiple stems are highlighted with green pencil, which accents them and ties them to the colors in the flowers and leaves.

Dave Brethauer

DOUBLE COLOR

One simple way to create interest is by applying two colors of ink to one stamp. You can use brush markers or small inkpads. The ink from pigment pads is more opaque than ink from the markers. If you don't want the background to be visible within the image, it's best to use pigment ink. If you want the background to show as a decorative element, work with markers. When working with markers, you may need to exhale (with a huff!) onto the stamp to moisten the surface after inking and before stamping.

We give you instructions on how to create the first of these three cards. The same technique is used for all three. Start by working with the lighter color first. To apply the ink, hold the stamp, rubber side up, and apply the color to the raised portions of the design. Work with only one color at a time. It's important to work quickly so that you stamp before the ink dries on the stamp's surface.

Creating the Project

1. Stamp the large, background thank-you stamp on your white cardstock. Ink your color block stamp and stamp it over the background (this stamp has narrow, white, horizontal lines throughout).

2. Clean the deckle-edge stamp well and apply dark-brown ink to the four outside edges. Stamp to create the border around the central panel.

3. Apply brick-red pigment ink to the flowers of the flower stamp. Then apply the olive-green ink to the stem portion of the stamp. Stamp the flowers in the center of the frame.

4. Trim, leaving a white border. Mount the design on brown cardstock and then mount onto your card. Stamp your greeting or sentiment below.

Lara Zazzi

16

BLOCKS OF COLOR

Color blocks, stamped in an orderly or random pattern, can enhance lettering and embellishments or create overall background patterns. Color-block stamps come in all shapes and sizes. Apply color each time you stamp, or apply color once and stamp two or three times to get subtle gradations of color in your designs. Remember that working in uneven numbers is a basic principle of good design.

BACKGROUND COLOR

One stamp—inked with the same color—is stamped several times across the surface of cardstock to ground the design. Some of the shapes overlap the edges of the paper to create a feeling of movement and depth. A few additional shapes—large solid and concentric circles and small squares and rectangles—are added in the same way. Buttons of bright, playful colors are glued at the centers of some of the circles to add further dimension.

Creating the Project

1. Stamp a square color block at the center of your note card to create the central flower pot.

2. Stamp the same block twice more, positioning one to either side of the center block and about ¼ inch above it.

3. Stamp the same block twice more, loosely aligning the tops of these outer blocks with the top of the center pot.

4. Ink the letters one at a time and stamp one in each background block.

5. Lay a piece of a paper over the top of each block as a mask. With brush markers, color the flower and the stem. Stamp each flower to "plant" it in the pot. Remove the mask. Be sure to clean the stamp before changing colors.

Hero Arts

A SOFT TOUCH

*S*tamping can be combined with different embellishments and papers to create simple yet sophisticated cards. We've used the same color inks and a touch of translucent vellum on these next few projects: a vellum tag is stamped with a snowflake; stamped lettering on a vellum envelope becomes a decorative element for the gift card; cardstock wrapped with vellum and embellished with glitter creates a soft, dreamlike effect for a baby card.

Creating the Project

1. Choose three different snowflake stamps. Stamp one snowflake across the background of the card with white ink. Stamp another with blue ink. Stamp the third stamp in the same color blue onto a vellum tag.

2. Attach the tag to the card with a blue eyelet. Thread a ribbon through the eyelet. Wrap the ribbon around the top of the card and tie a bow at the front of the card.

Kim Smith

A Muse Art Stamps

Creating the Project

1. Stamp the celestial design on white rectangular cardstock. Cover the rectangle with white vellum.

2. Punch a hole in the top center of the note card and insert a brad. Bend a short length of wire around the brad. Tape the ends to the front of the card.

3. "Hang" the card by mounting it with foam-mounting pads. Position it so that it covers the wire ends on the front of the card.

4. Add a little glitter glue to highlight the designs. Stamp a greeting or title onto the card.

Creating the Project

1. Stamp the bouquet image onto colored cardstock. Freehand cut out the shape, loosely following the outline.

2. Mount the shape on patterned paper. Mount the patterned paper onto complementary colored cardstock.

3. Punch a hole at the top of the card through all the layers. Thread a ribbon pull through the hole. Stamp the sentiment or greeting on the front of the vellum sleeve.

Petite Motifs

Creating the Project

1. Working on cardstock, randomly stamp a birthday bugle stamp in a single color to create an overall background.

2. Fold a piece of complementary-colored cardstock to create a pocket. Stamp a birthday cake on the front and the message "You're Invited."

3. Stamp several oak-tag shipping tags with different headings to provide details about the birthday event: time, place, and the guest of honor.

4. Stack the tags and attach a ribbon pull through the holes at the top. Inset the bundle into the pocket.

Kim Smith

Creating the Project

1. Stamp a light blue block on white cardstock. Stamp a darker blue striped block over the light blue block.

2. With the dark brown pigment ink, directly ink the "onesie" stamp. Center the design on the blue-striped background.

3. Trim the cardstock, leaving a white border. Mount the design on two-toned cardstock. Stamp your sentiment or greeting.

Cindi Nelson

THE PERFECT DETAIL

*S*imple designs can turn into elegant cards as soon as you add a few well-chosen decorative papers, inks, and other simple embellishments. Texture, shading, and pattern are all powerful design tools. Don't be afraid to combine stamping with other techniques and materials—with a little imagination, you can create a variety of special effects to perfectly suit every occasion.

Penny Black

Dave Brethauer

Creating the Project

1. Stamp the appropriate saying and image onto cream linen cardstock.

2. Stamp the bird and apply watercolor of a darker hue to the inside areas to shade. Color the insides of the leaves with watercolor or a pen.

3. Attach the cardstock to a gold-foil cardstock mat by inserting red eyelets in each corner.

4. Mount a rectangle of marbleized paper onto solid-red cardstock. Layer the pieces onto the green note card.

5. Apply dots of red glitter glue to form the berries. Be sure to allow the glue to dry thoroughly—about 15 minutes—before inserting the card in an envelope.

Creating the Project

1. In the upper third of the card, stamp the little bird.

2. Cut a mask to cover the bird's body. Stamp a bright green color block over the masked bird. Without re-inking, stamp another block a block's width away.

3. Clean the stamp and ink it with a darker green. First, stamp lightly on scrap paper to remove excess ink. Then stamp the card, adding a dark green block between the two bright green blocks.

4. Repeat to add two more blocks to each end to complete the row of five blocks.

5. Remove the mask from the bird and color it with bright-red colored pencils. Stamp "Merry Christmas" below your design.

THEMED ACCENTS

Add decorative accents with an extra detail—a ribbon, bunch of flowers, or a grommet—to give dimension to the design and make it uniquely your own. These three simple Valentine cards are enlivened by the addition of colorful embellishments appropriate to the holiday. "Valentine Wishes" incorporates red paper roses that are tied with a striped ribbon. "Happy Valentine's Day" is made with a mesh background stamp, flower stamps, a lettering stamp, and two, shiny, silver brads. The sophisticated heart card is stamped with gold metallic ink.

TIP

A little goes a long way. Try a single stamped motif to create a set of note cards with matching envelopes.

Cindi Nelson

happy valentine's day

Cindi Nelson

valentine wishes

Cindi Nelson

BY THE SEA

*T*he paper craft techniques in these two specialty note cards evoke the rushing water, rising waves, and sandy beach of the seashore. Torn paper, watercolor washes, and natural tones and materials all support the mood and theme of the designs—all work together to convey the feeling of the sea. Both cards are constructed in the same way, but in the smaller card, two square eyelets instead of punched holes are used to thread the sheer ribbon.

Creating the Projects

1. With a pigment ink or clear embossing fluid, ink the stamp and stamp it onto sand-colored, textured paper.

2. Apply white embossing powder to the wet ink. Shake off the excess and heat with a heat tool to melt.

3. Create a soft shadow around the shell with a watercolor wash. Tear the edge of the sand-colored paper to create a textured edge.

4. Cut pieces of two different shades of handmade or mulberry paper to the same width as the textured paper.

5. Tear the edges of the handmade papers to create soft frayed ends, offsetting their lengths slightly. Layer the papers and attach them to the card, wrapping the ends over the fold.

6. Punch two holes in the top of the card and the overlays and thread with a ribbon or raffia. Before tying the bow, attach a vellum square.

7. Tear the bottom front edge of the card and back with another sheet of torn mulberry paper to create a soft ragged edge.

RAINBOW EFFECTS

A rainbow pad is an inkpad that has several bands of different color ink on the same pad. You can create a subtle rainbow effect by inking one stamp with all the colors—or if you choose a rainbow pad with a more muted palette, as in the note card here, you can create a gradation of shades within a family of colors to produce a soft, muted effect. When working with a rainbow pad, clean the stamp between stampings so as not to contaminate or blur the colors. Simply pat the stamp with a damp paper towel.

Printworks

DRAMATIC DARKS

By stamping on a dark—rather than a light-colored—paper you can increase your opportunities for dramatic visual effects. You can stamp sparingly to allow the dark background to dominate the design. Or you can allow sections of the background to show through for a controlled effect—such as a dark outline or defined shape. Stamp the image with a watermark ink or an ink that is close to the color of the paper.

Creating the Projects

1. To make the card or the cover of the small book, stamp the design that you want to feature.

2. Outline the shapes freehand with colored pencil. Color in small details of the image. Or color the interior areas of the design, leaving only a narrow outline of the background paper to create a defining edge.

3. Trim and mount the design to a slightly larger piece of cardstock.

4. Center the cardstock on your notecard or book cover.

Nathalie Métivier

Nathalie Métivier

A SIGNATURE TOUCH

*B*y combining journaling with hand-cut shapes and decorative papers, you can add a warm, personal touch to your projects. You can also tailor their message to the occasion, the recipient, or your mood. If you would like to try a quick and easy alternative to handwriting, you'll be happy to learn that there are many decorative stamps available with preprinted messages in a variety of specialty shapes.

Adrienne Kennedy

Creating the Project

1. To make the LOVE card, below, fold a piece of solid-colored cardstock to create a note card. Cut two rectangles of decorative paper—one solid and one patterned—to mount to the front of the card.

2. With a pigment ink or clear embossing fluid, ink the O and V tag-shaped sentiment stamps and stamp each one onto the center of the patterned paper—at a diagonal to each other, as shown. (When finished, the stamped word "LOVE" will form a rectangle.) Apply gold embossing powder to the wet ink. Shake off the excess and heat with a heat tool to melt.

Adrienne Kennedy

3. On a separate piece of pink paper or cardstock, stamp and emboss the L and V.

4. Freehand cut the stamped sentiments into tag shapes.

5. Punch a hole in the top of two tags, and thread with decorative cords, tied with a slip knot.

6. Apply foam-mounting tape to the reverse side of the embossed "tags." Remove the backings and position them next to the letters stamped on the note card, to complete the word "LOVE."

7. Thread a small pink button with a short length of wire on the O "tag." Pierce the patterned and solid sheet with the wire and bend the ends open to secure it. Tape the ends to the back of the paper.

8. Mount the patterned sheet to the solid gold paper and then mount the gold paper to the front of the card.

9. Add four, old-fashioned-style photo corners to the patterned sheet to add the finishing touch.

Creating the Project

1. Layer two rectangles of complementary paper in graduated sizes to create a decorative mat. Attach the sheets to the front of your note card with four, old-fashioned-style photo corners.

2. With black ink, stamp two dragonfly-shaped sentiments on decorative printed text-weight paper or cardstock. Freehand cut out the shape, following the general line of the printing.

3. Mount the dragonflies onto a contrasting cardstock. Freehand cut the cardstock, following the general shape of the dragonflies and leaving a narrow border.

4. Apply small squares of mounting tape to the wrong side of the dragonflies, positioning the squares on the ends of each wing and at the bottom end of the body so that the narrow pieces are supported.

5. Remove the backing from the tape. Arrange the dragonflies at a jaunty angle to each other on the front of the card.

Adrienne Kennedy

Adrienne Kennedy

Creating the Project

1. Select or make a decorative square envelope. Mount it on two pieces of complementary or contrasting cardstock.

2. With black ink, stamp a heart-shaped sentiment on decorative printed text-weight paper or cardstock. Freehand cut out the shape, following the general line of the printing.

3. Mount the heart onto a contrasting background and freehand cut, following the shape and leaving a narrow border.

4. Attach the top portion of the heart to the top of the flap of the envelope.

5. Arrange a few paper flowers in the V of the heart.

STAMP AND VARIATIONS

With a little creativity, you can entirely change the look of a single stamp to produce a wide range of special effects. Here are three variations on a single stamp that make a lovely coordinated set for a special occasion—yet each also stands beautifully alone.

Creating the Project

1. Fold a wide strip of colored cardstock to make a "Thank You" note. Mount a contrasting or complementary textured paper to the front.

2. On white cardstock, stamp the chrysanthemum with a complementary-colored ink. Color the flower's center and petals with colored pencils.

3. Turn a tag punch upside down over the stamped image so you can see the image. Crop your design to the area you want to feature and punch out the tag.

4. Cut a rectangle of bright-colored paper to mount the tag. Punch a hole through the top of the tag and the mounting paper. Align the holes and glue the tag onto the paper.

5. Thread a colored ribbon through the holes and tie a bow. Glue the mounted tag to the front of the card.

Kim Smith

Creating the Project

1. Fold a horizontal strip of dark brown paper in half to create a note card. Mount a square of light blue on the front of the card.

2. Cut a slightly smaller square of brown and another, smaller square of blue. Mount the square to the front of the note card.

3. With a pigment ink or clear embossing fluid, ink the chrysanthemum stamp and stamp onto the smaller blue square. Apply brown embossing powder to the wet ink. Shake off the excess and heat with a heat tool to melt.

4. Punch holes through all the paper layers at the top center of the card.

5. Thread blue and brown ribbon through the holes, leaving the ends free on the front of the card.

Stacey Turechek

Kim Smith

Creating the Project

1. Stamp the chrysanthemum stamp several times on a piece of gold paper. Trim the paper to crop the design. By allowing the shapes to run off the edge of the paper, you create the sense of a continuing design.

2. Mask the flower shapes with masking material. Working direct to paper, color the background with a Cat's Eyes® or small inkpad.

3. Remove the masks. Color the flower centers and the tips of the petals with the Cat's Eyes® or inkpads to soften the effect.

Kim Smith

INK-EMBOSSING

*H*ere is a sparkling ink-embossed holiday card for Christmas. By adding a bit of embossing powder to a rubber-stamped image, you can create a fast and simple variation on the classic paper-embossing techniques.

Creating the Project

1. Layer two rectangles of complementary-colored paper in graduated sizes to create a decorative mat. Attach them to the front of your note card with four, old-fashioned-style photo corners.

2. With a pigment ink or clear embossing fluid, ink the ornament-shaped sentiment stamp and stamp it onto dark green cardstock or text-weight paper. Apply gold embossing powder to the wet ink. Shake off the excess and heat with a heat tool to melt. Freehand cut out the shape, following the general line of the printing.

3. On the reverse side of the ornament, place small squares of foam-mounting tape. Remove the backing from the adhesive and position the ornament.

4. Attach a fiber bauble at the neck of the ornament. "Pop" or glue a cancelled holiday stamp to the front of the ornament. For the finishing touch, tie a festive bow around the neck of the ornament.

Adrienne Kennedy

MOSAIC FRAME

*S*tamped papers can be cut and arranged in a variety of geometric shapes to create mosaic patterns, quilt patterns, or abstract designs. This technique is especially effective to decorate a frame that will feature a favorite photograph. To make the process fast and easy, you can work with self-adhesive sheets. This delightful frame was made from a Magenta Mosaic Frame Kit.

Creating the Project

1 Create five bands of random color and pattern on an 8½ x 11-inch self-adhesive sheet. With Cat's Eyes®, apply the color direct to paper. Choose contrasting and complementary shades.

2 Stamp each band of color with decorative, repeating patterns in harmonious colors. If you'd like, enhance some of the details with colored pencils. Cut the first patterned strip from the self-adhesive sheet. Remove the paper backing.

3 Randomly cut small triangular pieces. Hold the pieces on your fingertips until you are ready to use them. After you have cut several pieces, position a few on the frame mat to form a few clusters of fanlike designs.

4 When you have arranged all the pieces from the first strip, cut triangular pieces from the second strip and add them to the design. When the first color is finished, complete the

process with the 4 remaining colors to fill in the spaces. Fill in the empty areas around the frame with more fanlike clusters. Complete the design by randomly positioning pieces cut from the remaining strips. In this project, small lavender and cherry-red triangles were used to accent the blacks and green that are predominant in the photograph.

Blank self-adhesive plainstock sheets are great fun to work with. Coloring and cutting different size shapes, and then creating a pattern with those shapes offers endless possibilities.

This pattern is intricate, and it takes hundreds of small triangles to create the mosaic, but the craft is infectious. Try it. You'll have fun!

Nathalie Métivier

29

ONE STAMP, MANY USES

Create a garden of designs with a single stamp by varying the color of ink, the color of the paper, the section of the stamp used—or even the objects themselves. You can coordinate gift wrap, note cards, and place cards with a single stamp and color scheme to create an elegant presentation for any special event. The three-dimensional blossoms created from an extra stamped image add interest and texture. One stamp and a little imagination can offer wonderful creativity.

Kim Smith

Creating the Project

1. Cut a piece of paper large enough to wrap your package. (Don't waste time stamping paper you will not use.)

2. Ink your hydrangea stamp with two colors of brush pens—one color for the blossoms and one for the stems and leaves.

3. Randomly stamp the entire surface of the paper, leaving fairly even intervals between images. Vary the direction of the motif so that when the package is wrapped, some of the stamped images will read right side up. Wrap your gift.

4. To create the gift tag, stamp one hydrangea on three pieces of white cardstock.

5. Freehand cut one of the images. Fold a piece of cardstock of complementary color in half. The cardstock should be the approximate width of the shape.

6. Mount the cut-out flower, aligning the top of the image with the fold. Freehand cut the colored cardstock to the stamped shape, leaving a narrow border. Do not cut through the fold.

7. From the remaining two stamped images, cut out 13 individual blossoms. Gently pinch all four petals of each blossom to slightly curl up the ends. Place a dot of glue on each blossom and place them on top of the stamped tag.

8. Punch a small hole through the top of the folded card and tie a sheer ribbon around the package. Before tying the bow, thread the gift tag onto the ribbon.

Kim Smith

Creating the Project

1. To create the "Thank You" card, stamp three hydrangeas on the surface of your note card.

2. Trim the edge of the card so that the design seems to spill off the edges of the surface.

3. Mask each cluster of hydrangea blossoms. Color the background with a Cat's Eyes® inkpad or other small inkpad. Apply and blend several closely related colors to create a mottled, shaded effect. Remove the masks.

4. Color a few hydrangea stems with a bright-green colored pencil. Stamp the message and mount the card on two layers of complementary-colored cardstock.

Creating the Project

1. Cut a piece of colored cardstock to create each rectangular place card.

2. Stamp once along the edge of the front of each card to create a straight border of hydrangea blossoms, using only the top portion of the stamp.

3. Mask the stamped area. Then stamp again to continue the border.

Kim Smith

4. Lift the mask and reposition it over the newly stamped area. Be sure to align the edges of the mask and the image. Stamp another repeat. Continue masking and stamping until you've completed the entire border of the card.

5. Cut a narrow rectangle out of white cardstock for each card. Center the rectangle on the card to provide a space in which you can handwrite the guest's name. (Or, you can type or print out all the guests' names on white paper.)

Lady bug, lady bug...

PUNCH ART

No other paper craft leads you to expect such great things from a tiny scrap of paper than punch art! A paper punch is really just a small paper cutter, but with these simple handheld tools, available in every size, you can punch just about anything you can think of—hearts, houses, daisies, dragonflies, ribbons, roses, and more.

Even the simplest punched shapes have a lot of potential. The geometrics—squares, triangles, ovals, circles of varying sizes—will come in handy in unexpected ways. You can punch windows in photo frames to reveal smiling faces or punch a colorful patchwork quilt to warm up a "Welcome!" note. Punched triangles, circles, hearts, and squares also make wonderful confetti to sprinkle on the tops and sides of gift packages. Or fill a glassine envelope or cellophane pouch with colorful shapes and incorporate it into a scrapbook page or a festive party invitation.

There is no waste! Those scrap pieces left over after you have punched out your shapes are extra "found" tools. You can use these "negative" shapes as stencils, embossing templates, or die cuts within the same design—or in other designs another day.

PUNCHING

*Y*ou don't need to have a lot of different punches to get started. One simple punched shape may be just the accent you need whether you're creating a paper collage or a special scrapbook page. You can also repeat a single punched shape to form playful borders around a note card or to frame an elegant handwritten message.

A circle can become two or three flower petals, for example. Another way to create a dramatic effect is by cutting multiples of the same shape in half and rearranging them as "mirror" images in contrasting textures or shades. Experiment. It's quick and easy—and fun!

PUNCH ON PUNCH

*P*unches may look like simple tools, but they are so versatile and can yield a wide assortment of finished effects. Overlapping, interlocking, or alternating the direction of the shapes adds interest to a design. Punching multiple shapes in the same color creates a subtle, monochromatic motif. Punched papers of contrasting colors and patterns can be featured in a central design or cut into smaller, different shapes. Here are just three samples of what punches can do. The first project features a simple punched shape used alone. The second features a punched negative shape that has been combined with color, embellishments, and the special effects of a heating technique. The third project features a combination of layered punched shapes that have been arranged to form a delicate, decorative design.

In this project we punched the butterflies from lightweight cardstock and colored them using Cat's Eyes® pigment ink before attaching them to the punched tag. Notice that we attached only their bodies to the tag so that the wings are free and can lift slightly from the surface. A metal ring attached to the top of the tag adds an additional three-dimensional touch.

TIP

If your punches start to dull, punch through aluminum foil to resharpen them. Be sure you have some wax paper handy, too, and punch through it occasionally to keep your punches slick and smooth so they won't stick.

Creating the Project

1. Position your sunflower punch over the top edge of the front of a white cardstock note card. Punch out the shape.

2. With a larger circle punch, punch a circle of yellow printed paper. Place the circle on the inside cover behind the sunflower shape to add color.

3. Mix small dabs of brown and ochre liquid appliqué to create the center of the sunflower.

4. Heat the area from behind the card with a heating tool to raise the design.

5. Attach paper leaves and a small fabric ribbon.

Creating the Project

1. Partially ink a twin-flower stamp with black ink so that only the frame, stems, and leaves have color.

2. Punch yellow paper with a wavy square punch.

3. Punch white paper with a slightly larger white wavy square punch.

4. Punch two daisies out of white paper. Shape the petals by curling them upward slightly with your fingers.

5. Punch small flower centers for each daisy.

6. Color the stems and leaves with colored pencil.

7. Tie a love knot with a length of striped ribbon and attach it below the central design.

THINKING OUTSIDE THE BOX

*P*hotographs are the most important part of a scrapbook page. Select colors from the photos when choosing background papers and accents. You can also get ideas from the special occasion or event. The bunny head punch was used to create the whole bunny. A little imagination goes a long way!

Kim Smith

Easter Egg Hunt 2004

This was your first Easter egg hunt with cousin Mackenzie and sister Exa. The Easter Bunny marked your eggs with a "P" for Parker and filled them with Teddy Grahams. You weren't sure what to do at first, but after the first egg was opened, you got into the fun. When you had eaten all the Teddies, you brought the empty eggs to Aunt Jamie for a refill.

Parker Eugene Ritchie
17 months

Creating the Project

1. Working with various colors of paper, dry emboss a flowerpot and flowers with brass templates. Loosely cut along the edges of the embossed designs.

2. Create a journaling block. Cut a mat for the block.

3. Emboss blades of grass along the bottom of the mat, and cut around the outline of the embossing with a sharp knife. Tuck punched egg shapes and the journaling block behind the grass.

4. Punch five bunny heads. Turn one head to form the bunny's body. Cut ears from another head to form arms. Cut another ear to form the flowerpot bunny's waving arm.

5. Freehand cut the interiors of all the ears from colored paper.

6. Decorate the bunny using a marker and chalk.

The polka-dot pumpkin for this note card is really an apple punch. The paper color instantly changes the apple into a pumpkin and creates an unmistakable Halloween theme.

Creating the Project

1. Punch nine squares out of five cardstock colors. Make additional squares out of whichever colors you like best.

2. Glue the squares to a sheet of solid paper. Position the first square in the upper left corner. Use the straight edge of the paper as a guide to be sure the finished square is straight. Trim off the excess paper.

Kim Smith

3. Lay the nine-square block upside down on top of a texture plate (a hard plastic template with ridges). Rub the paper with wax paper. Run a stylus or embossing tool along the grooves of the textured plate to transfer the texture to the paper.

4. Lay the block on a dense foam pad or cutting mat. With a metal ruler and ponce wheel or perforator, faux-stitch eight rows. "Stitch" along the entire length of the block, working about ¼ inch from all four outside edges and ¼ inch from each "seam" between the squares.

5. Cut four strips of a dark-colored paper with a scalloped paper trimmer. To create a mitered effect, cut both ends of two of the strips at an angle. Glue the cut strips on top of the uncut strips to form a square frame.

6. Attach the nine-square block to the frame.

7. Working on the foam pad or mat, pierce a hole with an awl, piercing tool, or needle in each scallop of the scalloped edge of the strips.

8. Mount the block and frame to the front of the note card.

9. Punch out oak leaves and attach them to some of the squares—arranging them to create a fluttering effect. Note that we "flopped" some of the leaves—a good reason to use paper that has the same finish on each side.

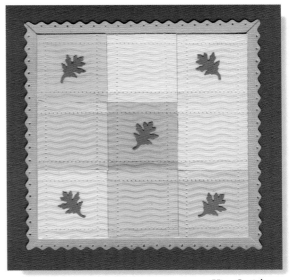

Kim Smith

A FRAME IN BLOOM

*E*ven the simplest punched shapes can be layered, cut, colored, and combined to create complex designs. When planning a layered punch-art design, think about the shapes you will need to create the object you have in mind. Before heading to the store, look closely at the punches you already own. By trimming pieces or halves of a punched shape, you can entirely transform its appearance—and add to the endless possibilities of what you can create.

Creating the Project

1 For each large flower, punch two large daisies from yellow cardstock and brown cardstock. Layer the flowers and add a brown medium flower for the center. For the half flowers, cut the large punched flowers in half and layer them, adding a snipped acorn for the center. Lightly shade the petals by applying brown chalk onto the ends with a Q-tip or cosmetic sponge.

2 To form the larger leaves, punch green cardstock with a snowflake punch and cut the shapes into three pieces.

3 To form smaller leaves, portions of a snowflake are tucked under a few of the petals. Small pink and blue flowers are punched and layered with small leaf shapes.

COLORS THAT WORK

*R*ed and green are complementary colors on the color wheel—which means that they create a natural balance when used together. The same is true of the various shades of red and green—which is why their pastel cousins look so lovely together. Pink and green make a vibrant and exciting twosome. Be sure to consult a color wheel when planning your designs. It just may lead you in an unexpected, bright, new direction.

Creating the Project

1. On a light-colored textured cardstock, stamp three rows of three leaves and stems.

2. Punch flower heads with ⅛-inch and ¹⁄₁₆-inch circle punches and a small flower—to show the budding bloom in progress.

3. With squares of foam-mounting tape, mount the design on a bright paper to add color to the flowers.

4. Mount the design to the front of the note card. Stamp your message below.

Creating the Project

1. Punch four decorative corner punches into colored cardstock. Mount the sheet onto the front of a note card.

2. Punch two large flowers in two different shades of the same color.

3. Attach a length of ribbon to a rectangle of white cardstock to form the flower stem. Position the punched flowers at the top.

4. Add spiral glitter stickers. Notice that the open swirl of the spirals mirrors the lacy open shapes of the corner punches. Position two different-sized stickers to form the leaves and one large sticker to form the flower's center.

Katrina Cunningham

40

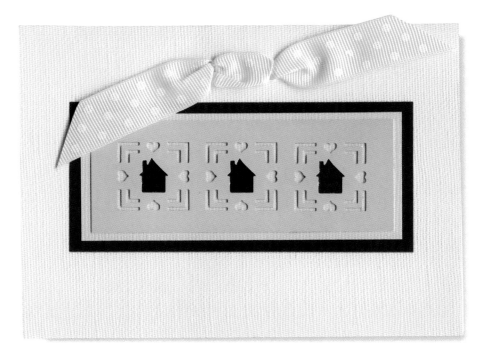

Creating the Project

1. The central design is made with a quilt punch, punched three times. To make sure the three shapes are aligned, insert the paper all the way into the punch each time.

2. Trim the edges of the paper to create an even border around the design.

3. Mount the strip on two layers of complementary-colored cardstock.

4. Punch the design in a contrasting color. Glue the punched house pieces in the opening of the squares. Punch two holes in the top front of the note card and thread with a decorative ribbon.

TIP

Punch squares or other shapes to create "windows" to display patterned papers, punched shapes, original artwork, or photos.

Creating the Project

1. Punch a scalloped-edge rectangle in the front of the card.

2. Punch the dress in a patterned paper and outline the edges with brown marker. Attach a small paper flower at the waist.

3. Center the dress in the window and mount it to the inside of the card with foam-mounting tape.

4. Freehand cut a rectangle in the same paper used for the dress. Cut a smaller rectangle from the scrap piece you punched out of the note card.

5. Stamp your greeting on the smaller rectangle. Mount both pieces and add a paper flower accent.

Kim Smith

A GARDEN OF POSSIBILITIES

*I*t seems that flowers can be made with just about every type of punch—from snowflakes to pinwheels to swirls. It's especially nice to mix and match shapes, varying their arrangement to create different effects. Paper patterns, textures, and colors are also an important feature in producing a unique end result. Even when projects rely on the same color palette, as seen here, you can create a wide range of designs through your choice and placement of decorative details.

Creating the Project

1. Stamp the tall stalk of flowers on rectangular white cardstock.

2. Paint with watercolor to fill in the stems and leaves.

3. To create dimensional flowers, punch several pieces in three shades of lavender paper with a pom-pom punch and small circle punches. Punch four white snowflakes. Layer the pieces to create flowers and attach to the card.

4. Tear a rectangle of textured cardstock against the edge of a deckled ruler to create straight but irregular edges.

5. Mount the floral design onto the torn backing and mount the backing to the front of the note card.

6. Knot a striped twill ribbon and attach it to the card as a side border.

Creating the Project

1. Punch a large scalloped circle out of vellum. Fold and overlap the edges of the circle to create a triangular wrap for your punched flower bouquet.

2. Cut a length of ribbon and attach it to the front of the note card.

3. Position the wrapped vellum on top of the ribbon. Bring the ribbon to the front and tie.

4. Punch eight white flowers. Punch eight yellow centers with a small circle punch.

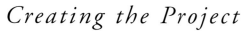

42

5. Insert the stems of several paper leaves into the folded vellum paper.

6. Arrange the flower blooms so they appear to form a bouquet. Mount some of the flowers on squares of foam-mounting tape to "pop" them from the surface of card.

A spiral shape makes a compelling central design. It draws the eye with its swirling motion on this note card and reinforces the shape of the metal tag. The top of a tomato-punched shape accents the spiral's center, and a tiny diamond chip adds sparkle. The tag is tied, but not glued—so it swings freely.

Creating the Project

1. Punch a square window in the front of your note card.

2. Punch a second square of the same size from colored cardstock. Attach the colored square inside the card so that it shows through the punched window.

3. Punch the dragonfly in two different colors of cardstock. Glue one dragonfly to the top of the note card so that it appears to be flying over the window.

4. Cut the second dragonfly's body away from the wings. Glue the second body on top of the first to change the color and add depth and dimension.

TIP

Keep a pair of tweezers nearby if you are working with small punched shapes—they will make it easier for you to handle the small paper pieces.

DOUBLE DELIGHT

*I*f you have a favorite design, there's no reason why you can't use it over and over again. Simply vary the colors, shapes, and patterns to suit any season or occasion. The bumblebee announcement doubles as a ladybug invitation just by changing from yellow to red, from stripes to dots! And the little ducks make the perfect birth announcement for a little boy or a little girl.

Creating the Project

1. To make the bumblebee card, punch corners in the front of your note card. Tuck a sheet of colored cardstock underneath the decorative flaps.

2. To make the ladybug card, hand-cut a tag to form three right angles—one at the top and one at each bottom corner. Position the corner punch at each right angle and punch the decorative shape. Mount the tag to the front of the card and insert a tag of patterned paper under the corners.

3. To make each insect, punch three insects— one in yellow (bumblebee) or red (ladybug) cardstock, one in black cardstock, and one in vellum.

4. Cut the head and a strip of the body from the black bee. Cut the head from the black ladybug and punch the spots with circle punches. Overlay those pieces on the appropriate insect.

5. Cut the vellum bodies in half to make wings.

6. Form curled antennae with short lengths of wire. Brads form the eyes.

7. Mount each insect on the card with foam-mounting tape. The ladybug message is stamped. The bumblebee journaling is computer-generated.

Lady bug, lady bug...

Here's the Buzz....

TIP

Q: When does a ladybug look like a bumblebee?

A: When it is yellow with a big-black stripe.

Look beyond the tools and shapes to created additional effects.

44

Creating the Project

1. Punch the body and head of each duck. Glue the pieces together.

2. Highlight the details and contours of the bill, wings, and body shape with chalk pastels.

3. Attach small brads to make the eyes.

3. To make the pink card, cut out the shape of the wing with a craft knife. Punch a large oval in patterned pattern and mount it to the front of the note card. Center the duck on the oval and mount it on a strip of foam-mounting adhesive. Attach a tiny ribbon to the tuft of feathers at the top of the duck's head.

4. To make the blue card, tear three sheets of vellum and a sheet of dark blue, textured cardstock to form waves. Attach them to the front of the note card. Tuck the duck behind one of the waves so he can swim away and attach him with a strip of foam-mounting adhesive. Stamp a metal-rimmed tag with your announcement. Punch a hole in the top of the card and attach the tag with a blue ribbon.

Creating the Project

1. Mount a large rectangle of patterned vellum to a bright pink note card. Mount a small rectangle of textured cardstock on the vellum.

2. Punch two shoes out of a deep pink cardstock.

3. Flop one of the shoes so that you have a right shoe and a left. Color the details with colored pencil or chalk. Glue tiny buttons to each of the "straps."

4. Mount the shoes next to each other on the pink rectangle.

A LITTLE SOMETHING EXTRA

*T*he photograph is the star of this scrapbook page. The color image was converted to sepia tone to give the page an old-fashioned feel and to neutralize the colors in the image itself—so they wouldn't conflict with the muted shades featured in the design. The journaling block is an essential component, as it should be on any scrapbook page. Embossing adds texture and dimension to the simplest shapes. There are so many little details that add interest and fun to your projects. Punching the little teddy bear in a second color and trimming it to create a shirt for him is one.

Learning to Be Nice

Your mom and dad created a special reading room for you. It's a small, very cozy space in the corner of the living room, between the couch and the floor lamp. In this little mini-library, you have your own small chair and a large stack of books. You go there often and love to look at picture books, pointing out the airplanes, trucks, cars, and diggers. Nonni loves this picture taken when Aunt Jamie caught you reading a book about how to be nice.

Parker Eugene Ritchie
18 months

Creating the Project

1. Mount your photograph and journaling block on cardstock and attach to your scrapbook page.

2. Working with a stencil, emboss the shape of the plane and the sailboat in a bright-colored cardstock. Lay each shape, right side up, on the texture plate. Run wax paper over the top of the paper so that the stylus or embossing tool will glide easily. Work with a straight-line template for the airplane to elongate the shape. Work with a wavy-line template for the sailboat to mirror the ocean waves.

3. Freehand cut around the embossed images. Attach them to the scrapbook page.

4. Punch out the blue stars and little cars and arrange them as accents on your design elements.

Creating the Project

1. Mount a piece of yellow cardstock to the front of your note card.

2. Dry emboss a slightly smaller piece of white cardstock with wave and sun stencils.

3. Add glitter glue to the crests of the waves. Mount the embossed sheet on the note card.

4. Dry emboss a sailboat in yellow cardstock. (Note that this is the same stencil as the one used on the scrapbook page, opposite, but there is no additional texture added.) Mount the sailboat to the embossed white sheet with a strip of foam-mounting tape.

5. Punch a small, blue, folk-art-style star. Attach it to the front of the sailboat with a small square of foam-mounting tape.

Creating the Project

1. Punch four decorative corners in the front of your note card.

2. Tuck a rectangle of colored cardstock beneath the corners.

3. Punch two teddy bears—one in brown paper and one in a colored, patterned paper.

4. Cut the top portion of the colored body and glue it to the brown body to create a small "shirt."

5. Punch a blue patterned star and add it to the center of the shirt.

6. Chalk the contours of the bear's tummy, head, and limbs with dark brown chalk.

7. Attach a heart-shaped brad to form the nose.

8. Add two dots with a glaze pen to make the eyes.

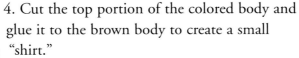

The edges of the small embossed squares are lightly sanded to soften and create a "weathered" look.

HAPPY FATHER'S DAY!

*W*hat to get the man who has everything? Why not start with an extra-special, one-of-a-kind greeting card. Handmade cards can be tailored to any occasion and to the interests and hobbies of the recipient. They say a lot about the maker, too, and add a personal touch that nothing else can. Punches make it fast and easy to put together last-minute packages, too—so don't forget to add a punched trimming and gift tag in coordinated patterns, colors, and themes.

Creating the Project

1. Punch out several flowers and leaves of the same design in various shades of cardstock.

2. With a fine-tipped marker, outline the outer edges of the petals, the flower centers, and leaves.

3. Cut off portions of some of the petals so it looks as though the flowers are gathered in a three-dimensional bouquet.

4. Stack the flowers on an oval piece of cardstock, gluing them into place.

5. Wrap a striped twill ribbon around your package. Attach the bunch of flowers to the top of the package with a strip of foam-mounting tape. This decoration is perfect for packages that need to be mailed. Although the design looks three-dimensional, it's actually flat and sturdy. The recipient can remove the decoration and save it for future use.

Creating the Project

1. Punch four dark squares and four, slightly smaller light-colored squares.

2. Attach a dark square to each side of your box.

3. Turn the light-colored squares to form diamonds and attach one to each dark square.

4. Punch two geckos and two Kokopelli shapes from dark cardstock. Alternating shapes, attach one to each light diamond.

5. Rather than wrap the entire box with ribbon, punch holes at the top and bottom of two opposite sides. Lace light and dark strands of raffia through the holes and tie them in a bundle at the top.

Kim Smith

e punched a circle out of brown cardstock and glued it inside a metal-rimmed tag. We then punched four different papers—one gold, one silver, and two shades of green—with the golf punch, which includes the grass, the golf club, golf balls, and tee. By selectively layering the various colors over appropriate parts of the golf punched base, we have created a colorful three-dimensional image on the free-swinging tag.

Creating the Project

1. Mount a square of dark-red paper slightly off center on the note card.

2. Stamp circles of various sizes with green ink on a smaller square of textured cream-colored cardstock.

3. Punch circles of various sizes in several of the green circles, varying the positions of the holes.

4. Mount the punched square on top of the red paper. The punched holes instantly become pimentos!

5. Stamp your cheery toast on the surface of your design. Stamp a martini cocktail and mount it to the card with foam-mounting adhesive.

Katrina Cunningham

MACKENZIE'S EASTER EGG HUNT

*P*ick up the colors in the image and let your decorative embellishments spill onto the photograph itself to make a lively and colorful design. One great photo, coordinated papers, and assorted punches in various shapes and sizes are all you need to make a memorable scrapbook page.

Easter Egg Hunt 2004

We celebrated Easter with Nonni, Bacha, Christie, Tim, Exa, and Parker. After Church, I couldn't wait to get back into my jeans and sneakers for the egg hunt. Even though we hadn't planted grass in our new yard, the Easter Bunny still hid eggs in the rock wall and bushes. He marked Parker's eggs with a "P" and hid them where they were easy to find. The eggs for Exa and I were much harder to find-and had better treats.

Mackenzie Joi Xia Kilmartin - 8 1/2 years

Creating the Project

1. Select an assortment of papers to match the colors and the feeling of the photograph you are featuring on your page. Select several embellishments that also match the spirit of the page—brads, spiral clips, punches.

2. Punch floral shapes in a variety of colors and sizes. Shade the edges and surfaces with pastel-colored chalks.

3. Mount a patterned paper on a decorative scrapbook page.

4. Mount your photograph and journaling block on two shades of complementary papers.

5. Layer the floral motifs around the central photo. Notice that this page has a three-dimensional feel—even though the embellishments are only modestly raised.

6. Add spiral-clip centers and decorative brads to the centers of some of the flowers. Add a small flower in the foreground of the photo and decorate your jounaling with spiral clips.

VARIATIONS ON A THEME

Decorative accents can take center stage for matching notecards, invitations, gift wrap, or packaging. Whenever you finish a project you particularly like, store all the extra papers and embellishments in one place, so you can easily find them when you're ready to create something new.

Creating the Project

1. To make this Japanese Wish Box, cut paper to 9 inches wide by 12 inches long.

2. Fold the 12-inch-length in half to create a 6 x 9-inch sheet.

3. Open and fold each end into the crease. (You will now have four 3 x 9-inch sections.)

4. Measure in 3 inches from the 12-inch side.

5. Score and fold. Repeat on the other side. (You will now have 12 3-inch-square sections.)

6. On the top, cut out the right and left squares, leaving the center square in place.

7. Round the bottom corners of the remaining square. This is the flap.

8. Fold the four corner squares of the box with an origami square fold.

9. Pull the triangles made by the squash fold to the front and back of the box and gently close.

Note: Use a bone folder to crease the folds. Adjust the size of the box as necessary. We made a paper band to hold the box closed by cutting a strip of paper 12 inches long and wrapping it around the box.

STICKER ART

*W*ait 'til you see what you can do with stickers! They seem so simple, don't they? Not much to them at all. Well, you have a treat in store. They may be simple to use, but once you see how they work—and play—together, you'll have new appreciation for the humble sticker.

There are sheets and rolls of stickers for every occasion—trees, fairies, kites, boxes, bears, you name it. Each one is colorful and fun on its own—but the secret to sticker art is what they can do together. All the materials and projects in this chapter are from Mrs. Grossman's Paper Company.

Mix and match sizes, colors, and themes. Arrange mirror images or layer complementary shapes to create cheerful three-dimensional scenes. You can also cut your stickers apart and reassemble them—or use just half!—to make even the simplest sticker work in a multitude of ways.

Stickers applied randomly over a surface sometimes create a flat—and often chaotic—design. By clustering or overlapping your stickers, you can give your artwork a sense of depth, create a more pleasing composition, and establish a strong focus that will draw the viewer's eye.

Just because stickers are so easy to use, it doesn't mean you should use too many. Consider the overall design of your card or page. Be sure to leave some negative space (empty areas around and between the stickers) to make the composition easier to read. Otherwise, those charming motifs that you are trying to feature may get lost in the shuffle.

SIMPLY ELEGANT

A simple gingko leaf sticker adds an elegant touch to note cards, gift tags, and packages. By simply varying the colors and textures, you can create entirely new moods and finished effects. Metallic papers, fiber ribbons, and mizuhiki cords all add dimension—and a touch of the exotic—to the subtle surfaces.

Mrs. Grossman's Paper Company

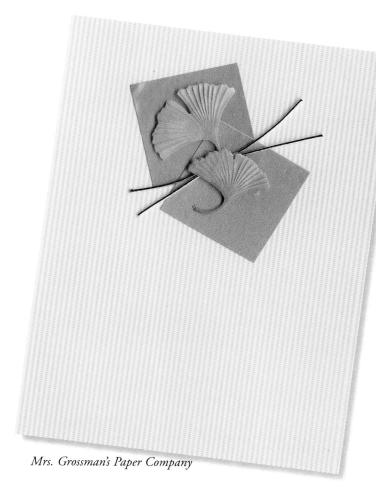

Mrs. Grossman's Paper Company

Two sticker squares, two gingko leaves, and two mizuhiki cords at jaunty angles are bound to make you feel good.

Creating the Project

1. Fold cardstock in half to create a 4 ½ x 6 ¼-inch card.

2. Tear long edges of vellum and place on the center of the card using small pieces of double-sided tape in the corners.

3. Cut one 2 x 2-inch square and two 1 x 1-inch squares of special paper. Affix the squares over the torn vellum.

4. Place the larger gingko sticker in the center and the smaller gingko sticker popped with foam tape overlapping it.

54

DECORATIVE BOXES

A simple sticker in a simple frame can make a beautiful and sophisticated presentation. Choose your colors and textures carefully to keep the look clean and elegant. Strong sticker images, layered papers, and decorative cords combine to produce an elegant but casual effect.

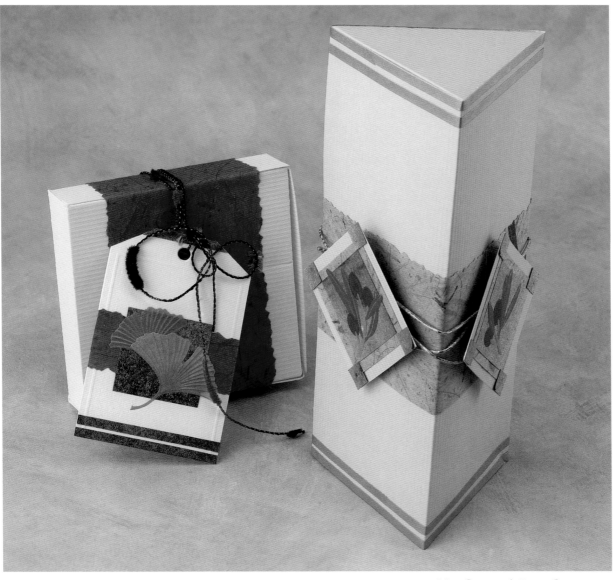

These two elegant boxes were made using templates found on page 124, and both boxes were wrapped with a band of color sticker paper trimmed with deckle-edge scissors. Added embellishments include mizuhiki cord, thin fiber cords, and metallic stickers, among others. The two examples have similar techniques, but different shapes and materials.

Mrs. Grossman's Paper Company

STICKERS ON STICKERS

*Y*ou can create three-dimensional sticker art by backing stickers with their duplicates—so that they read the same way from both sides. This clever little flowerpot make delightful note card to insert in a potted plant or wildflower bouquet.

Creating the Project

1. Using the template on page 124, cut out the flowerpot card from sturdy brown cardstock or lightweight board.

2. Cut two pieces of white cardstock to create the inside liner.

3. Add daisy flower stickers to the front of the card. Back the daisies with duplicate stickers.

4. Add the bee sticker. Back the bee with a duplicate sticker.

5. Glue both pieces of white liner to the inside of the card.

6. Tear the edges of two 1 x 3-inch rectangles of brown paper. Attach the rectangles to the outside of the pot with foam-mounting tape to form the flowerpot rim.

Mrs. Grossman's Paper Company

TIP

*I*f you are popping stickers—or positioning them to overhang the edges of the paper—you don't want them to stick where they're not wanted. Peel the sticker off its backing—or peel away half of the backing, depending on the effect you're creating. With your finger or a small brush, dab some talc, baby powder, or cornstarch on the portion of the sticker that is exposed. The powder will neutralize the adhesive—this way, the sticker won't stick to anything it isn't supposed to!

You may sometimes want a sticker to be viewed on both sides. If so, partially back the sticker (the part that will show) with an identical sticker, arranged as a mirror image. Place the adhesive side of the sticker on the page, and the illusion is complete (and neat)!

SPECIAL TOUCHES

*Z*igzag and ribbon stickers and specialty tags make it easy to add decorative touches to your note cards. Your artwork will have all the warmth, texture, and dimension of fabric embellishments—without any of the work of cutting and gluing.

Creating the Project

1. Make a note card of ribbed paper.

2. On the front of the card, attach zigzag strip line stickers, about 1 inch away from the right edge of the card front. Carefully trim away the excess note card with scissors.

3. Cut and fold a sheet of vellum so that it fits inside the card, matching both edges.

4. Place a daisy sticker on a textured tag. Do not remove the sticker lining. Place another daisy sticker on top of the first with foam-mounting tape. Powder any exposed adhesive surfaces.

5. Fold yellow line stickers in half lengthwise. Loop the design line through the hole in the tag. Trim excess length.

6. Remove the liner from the tag and position it on the front of the card.

TIP

*B*e sure to cut stickers while they are still on their backing paper. Otherwise, you'll be peeling stickers and adhesive off your scissors. They'll be easier to handle, too, and ready for sticking when you are.

Mrs. Grossman's Paper Company

Mrs. Grossman's Paper Company

PINWHEEL GIFT BOX

You may remember playing with pinwheels as a child. Well, they can be just as charming now that you're all grown up. By simply cutting and folding a decorative square, you can create a whimsical gift package for kids of all ages.

Creating the Project

1 Cut and assemble a box. The paper square for the pinwheel should be 1½ inches larger than the box. Adhere a sheet of patterned paper to the back of a sheet of ribbed paper. From each corner, cut along the diagonal of the square toward the center, stopping about ¾ inch from the center of the square. Punch a hole in each left corner of the four triangles you have cut in the square. Punch a hole in the center of the square.

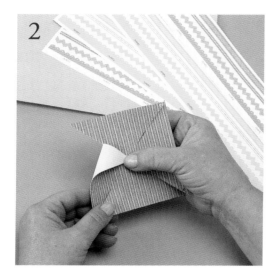

2 Fold a punched corner toward the center of the square and hold in place with your thumb.

3 Fold the remaining three corners to the center, aligning all the holes in the triangles and the square. Insert a long brad or small length of thin wire through the holes to secure the pinwheel.

4 Embellish with rickrack and add the pinwheel to the top of the package.

A GENTLE TOUCH

*F*abric stickers make it possible to quickly and easily create patchwork-quilt designs, ribbons, and bows. And what better place for a cozy and colorful fabric design than on a card for a new baby—whether it's a birth announcement, a gift card, or a party or christening invitation. The word "BABY" is die-cut and decorated with fabric-swatch stickers. The bow is made with fabric stickers, too. These same techniques can be adapted to create a gift-package decoration. These projects mix and match assorted vellum and fabric stickers and delicate pastel textured papers.

Mrs. Grossman's Paper Company

Creating the Project

1. With a die cutter and letter dies, punch the word "BABY" from pastel paper. Decorate the letters with fabric-swatch stickers.

2. Adhere the letters to a rectangle of paper. Mount the rectangle onto a slightly larger rectangle of colored paper.

3. To make the bow, cut a ¾-inch-long strip of line sticker with the backing still attached. This will wrap around the bow vertically. Cut an additional strip for the "ribbon." Make two loops in the middle of the ribbon to create a bow. Remove the backing from the ¾-inch-long strip and wrap it around the center of the loops to form the knot. Trim the ends of the ribbon.

4. Finish the card by attaching the decorative rectangle and the bow to the front of the card.

Crisscrossed pink line stickers wrap across the length and width of the top surface of a pillow box. Strips of blue-striped line stickers create the bunny's collar and a pearl dot creates the bunny's eye. The bunny, attached with foam-mounting tape, masks the intersection of the striped stickers.

Mrs. Grossman's Paper Company

ADDING DIMENSION

Mrs. Grossman's Paper Company

*F*oam-mounting tape gives the leafy wreath on this Thanksgiving greeting card extra depth and dimension. The photorealistic leaf stickers catch the light to create glossy surfaces and moody shadows. Randomly placed faceted accents draw the eye around the wreath and add to the festive feeling.

Creating the Project

1. Fold a sheet of special paper in half to create the note card.

2. Cut and fold a sheet of white paper of the same size and place it inside the card as a liner.

3. Cut a square of the colored sticker sheet. Mount the square on a square of black paper ¼ inch larger than the sticker.

4. Arrange fall leaves stickers to form a wide circle. Back some of the leaves with foam-mounting tape to add dimension. Powder any exposed areas of adhesive. Attach the wreath to the square. Finish by embellishing with gold dots.

5. Attach the design to the front of the card with foam-mounting tape. Trim the edges of the card with textured gold lines.

6. Add the journaling sticker below the design.

TORN VELLUM

Layers of torn vellum papers mirror the vellum leaf stickers to create a soft, airy background for this dragonfly card design. The realistic lines and details in the body and wings of the dragonfly sticker create a strong focal point, yet blend harmoniously with the rest of the design.

Mrs. Grossman's Paper Company

WINDOW BORDERS

A mixture of patterns, colors, and raised and textured surfaces all work together in this card to create the illusion of a stage set. And you thought stickers were flat! This whimsical Mother's Day card is the perfect greeting for Mom from one of her two-legged—or four-legged—"kids."

TIP

*Y*ou may sometimes want an overhanging image to be viewed on both sides of the paper. If so, partially back the sticker (the part that will overhang) with a mirror image sticker. Place the adhesive side of the sticker on the page, and the illusion is complete (and neat!) The puppy with the teapot sticker has a mirror-image sticker placed back-to-back to it on either side of the front window. When you open the card, you see the puppy and a teapot, not the back of the stickers.

Mrs. Grossman's Paper Company

Layers of popped and eye-popping colors make these holiday tags the perfect accessories to holiday packages or greeting cards. Fast and easy to make, you can give one to everyone on your list.

Mrs. Grossman's Paper Company

STATIONERY GIFT SET

*T*his entire stationery gift set is designed with a unified color scheme and repeating motifs and textures—but each component has its own surprising and unique feature.

Creating the Project

1. Cut a strip of sheer stickers. Trim one edge with deckle-edge scissors. Position it on a sheet of stationery. Center a large square of vellum over the deckled edge.

2. Mount two squares of textured tags on two squares of vellum and trim with the deckle-edge scissors. Center an orchid sticker in each textured tag square. Save one square for the note card. Position the other at a 45-degree angle on the vellum square on the letter paper. Place line stickers along the right edge of the stationery.

3. To make the note card, fold a sheet of paper in half. Line the lower inside flap with Blanc Papier Full Sheet. Trim the bottom edges with deckle-edge scissors.

4. Center a large rectangle of Blanc Papier along the top fold of the card. Trim the bottom edge with line stickers.

5. Cut off the end of a rectangular textured tag and center it on the line stickers.

6. Center a large vellum square on the end of the rectangle. Cut a length of texture tag and position one end above the vellum square. Wrap the other end over the fold. Adhere the tag square you made in Step 2 to the vellum square at a 45-degree angle.

7. The envelope is vellum. Add line stickers to the edge of the envelope flap. Add a small block sticker and an orchid sticker as a seal, to coordinate the envelope with the note card.

8. To make the place card, fold a sheet of paper in half. Place the large rectangular textured tag on a sheet of vellum and trim the edges with deckle-edge scissors.

9. Center a square tag at a 45-degree angle at the top of the rectangle. Trim the top of the tag with a strip of line stickers. Center an orchid in a small block sticker and then center the sticker on a small vellum sticker. Center the layers on the angled tag.

10. Attach the rectangle to the folded paper. To complete the place card, either powder the backs of the stickers that overhang the top of the card or back the stickers with duplicates.

Mrs. Grossman's Paper Company

BATTY HALLOWEEN CARD

*W*hat a delightfully ghoulish invitation to a Halloween bash! Complete with cobweb-draped windows, upside-down bats, and a lavender wash of night sky, this clever card is sure to delight trick-or-treaters of all ages.

Creating the Project

1. Cut or punch three small square windows of the same size, evenly spaced, in the front of the card. Cut three black frames with openings the same size as the square cut-outs. Cut three squares of mauve vellum slightly smaller than the frames and attach to the backs of the frames. Place bat stickers in each frame.

2. Cut three large spider-web stickers to fit over the edges of the windows. Attach the frames over the webs. Trim the top and bottom of each frame with lavender sliver stickers.

3. Cut a mauve liner for the card. Add small spider-web stickers to the edges. Decorate the lavender vellum envelope with alphabet stickers, bat stickers, and a Happy Halloween sticker.

SNOW SCENE POP-UP CARDS

*P*op-up cards seem like too ambitious a project? Not when you're working with stickers, they aren't. This entire winter scene was made with stickers, a few glittery accents, and some strategically placed double-stick tape. You can do this! Really. Go on, give it a try.

Creating the Project

1 Fold a sheet of paper in half to make the card. Fold a sheet of different colored paper in half to make

the inside lining of the card. Cut two sets of parallel lines in the liner, crossing the fold line, as indicated on the template. Fold the cutout strips toward you. Attach the lining to the inside of the card.

2 Position a portion of a winterscape sticker under the top edge of the

cutout section of the liner. Trim any excess overhang at the edge of the card. Beginning at the right-hand edge of the card, adhere the right half of the sticker on top of the first, positioning it slightly closer to the fold. Place tree stickers on the background and on the front folds of the cutouts. Powder the backs of the tree stickers.

3 Place penguin stickers in the right-hand tree. Back them with the reverse images of penguins. Cut the flipper of the penguin in the back-

ground so it can hold the strand of gold twine. Wrap and glue the gold twine around the left-hand tree. Run it under the penguin's flipper, around the right-hand tree, and along the "foreground" of the scene.

4 Attach decorative embellishments to the twine to create "lights." Trim the top and bottom of the card with striped line stickers. Decorate the front of the card and trim the top and bottom with blue line stickers. Place short strips of striped line stickers perpendicular to the blue stickers. Cut a tapered tag in half. Place the bottom half on a textured tag. Make a ribbon for the tag from pieces of striped line stickers. Attach the tag to the front of the card at a slight angle. Cut pieces of icicle stickers and hang them off the edge of the tag.

PAPER FOLDING

Decorative paper folding adds instant drama and dimension to paper craft projects. There are many types of paper folding. The best known is the ancient Japanese art and craft of origami. With just a few carefully placed folds, origami artists create three-dimensional objects of all levels of complexity—simple flower accents, square or octagonal gift boxes, elegant fans, and graceful crane and swan sculptures. Almost all can be made from a single piece of paper and a few basic folds—such as the four-corner fold, square fold, triangular fold—and variations.

Simple or intricate origami shapes make beautiful ornaments for the Christmas tree or decorative accents for the top of an extra-special gift package. Folded shapes also make wonderful frames for stand-alone portraits or for photographs featured on your scrapbook page. Simple accordion folds and pleating are essential to the paper crafter's repertoire—and they make it fast and easy to create folded books, cards, and photo albums. You can work with a variety of types of paper in a multitude of colors and patterns to achieve the three-dimensional effect and mood you want to create.

Tea bag folding is a Dutch technique for making interlocking shapes with paper squares of the same pattern to form frames, borders, or decorative central motifs. Iris folding, which also originated in the Netherlands, gets its name from the "eye" or "iris" of the shutter of a camera. Folded papers are arranged in a spiral pattern to create a central opening that appears to have multiple layers of open "shutters."

IRIS-FOLDED SQUARES

*T*he craft of iris folding gets it name from the "eye" or iris of the shutter of a camera. Folded papers are arranged in a spiral pattern to create a central opening—the iris—that appears to have layers of "shutters" around it. The effect creates the illusion of depth and dimension. And what better way to draw your eye to the "eye" than with a glittery bauble or mirrored surface placed in the center?

Creating the projects

1. Make a copy of the iris pattern. Cut or punch an opening—of the same size as the outermost square of the pattern—in the front of a piece of cardstock. Tape the card or cardstock, right side down, on top of the pattern so that the pattern shows through the window. (Note that because you are working from the back of the card, the pattern will be reversed on the front.)

2. Choose four different colors and patterns of lightweight decorative papers (try chiyogami, somegami, or another type of Japanese paper). Coordinate the papers with your cardstock. It's best to work with a solid rather than a patterned cardstock so as to focus all the attention on the iris-folded design. Cut two strips of each paper—¾ inches wide and about 8 to 10 inches long. Label the back of the strip pairs as A, B, C, and D. Fold a narrow (about ⅛ inch) hem along the length of each strip to the wrong side of the paper.

3. Lay one of the A strips over the area labeled 1A on the pattern, right side down, with the folded edge toward the center of the pattern. Cut the strip so that about ¼ inch or a little more overhangs the window on each end. Attach the strip to the back of the window with tape or glue stick.

4. Repeat the process, laying one of the B strips over the area labeled 2B. Continue laying down strips, following the numbered sequence of the pattern, matching the lettered papers to the lettered areas as indicated.

5. Before choosing the paper for the "iris," remove the design from the pattern and turn over the cardstock. Test a few different papers before deciding which paper to use.

6. If you are making a note card, cut and fold your cardstock. Mount the framed design directly on the card or decorative paper. Add a small ribbon or embellishment above or within the design.

SUPPORTING FORCES
Layering papers with a limited palette and interesting texture adds drama to any project. The deeper the colors and the more varied the textures, the more dramatic the finished effect will be. This iris-folded card is called, "Blue Ocean." Color, texture, and shape certainly communicate the idea.

Cherryl Moote

1. Choose four light weight decorative papers (like chiyogami) that co-ordinate with your color scheme. Cut two strips of each paper 3/4" wide and approximately 8"-10" long. Label the back of the strips A, B, C, D.

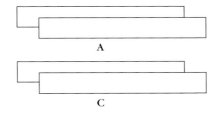

A

B

C

D

2. Fold in a narrow hem on each paper strip approximately 1/8" along the length to the wrong side of the paper.

3. Choose one strip from your A pile. Lay it over the number 1A on the pattern, good side down, folded hem edge to the center of the pattern. Cut a piece off the strip long enough that about 1/4" or a little more extends on either side of the cut out. Attach the strip to the back of the window with tape or glue stick. Using a B strip, repeat the step for the space labeled 2B. Continue in this manner.

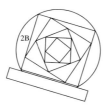

Instructions by Cherryl Moote

IRIS KITE CARD

By varying the size and shape of the opening, you can adapt the basic steps for creating an iris fold to make a pictorial design. This kite shape is simply an elongated diamond, cut with a metal straightedge and a craft knife. Four different patterned papers work within a simple blue-and-white color scheme. The palette and the patterns create a calm, high-contrast effect. The kite is mounted on a white background to enhance the sense of wide-open spaces and endless sky. The six small diamond shapes resemble miniature kites and echo the shape of the mirror-surface iris. The small kites can be punched or cut by hand. A length of nylon cord adhered to the surface of the card adds luster, dimension, and a realistic touch.

IRIS-FOLDED CRANE

The iris-folded wing of this dramatic and elegant crane was created with two patterned papers and a solid grey paper. The grey paper defines the inner, curved edge of the open wing and also forms the background that is visible through the cut stencil of the bird's body and opposite wing. The tone and sheen of the paper contribute to the formality of the design.

Cherryl Moote

70

IRIS-FOLDED HOLLY

*F*irst, the designer drew this iris-folded holly leaf so that she could plan the layout, size, and sequencing of the paper strips. Then she cut the shape freehand into the cardstock to form a window. The iris-fold design contains four shades of holiday-green papers with subtle, varying textures. The paper for the iris center is a heavy Japanese paper with an icy metallic sheen that adds a bit of seasonal sparkle. The second holly leaf is cut from the same paper but is folded and embossed to create "vein" textures on the surface. The cluster of red berries, cut from red velveteen paper, introduces a new shape and new texture—and cheerily grounds the design on the card.

Cherryl Moote

IRIS ORNAMENT

*T*his decorative bulb, created with spiraling strips of five vibrant papers, makes the most of contrasting and complementary colors. The colorful strips are arranged to draw the eye around the circle and directly into the glistening star-stickered center. A gold donut-shaped eyelet surrounds the punched hole at the top and is decoratively threaded with a nubby orange-silk ribbon. Although it has none of the traditional holiday colors, this beautiful design would make a beautiful card for Christmas—but it is also a stunning way to send a greeting for any other type of special occasion.

ORIGAMI INKWELL CARD

*O*rigami, the art of folding paper, is one of the oldest and most revered Asian art forms. Learn a few basic folds and you can create beautiful, magical paper figures. All you need is paper—any kind of fairly lightweight paper will do—wrapping paper, laser printer paper, magazine paper, as well as special origami paper. The one requirement is that the paper can be cleanly creased without tearing and that it have true right angles. You are limited only by your imagination—mix solid with patterned papers, light with dark, bright colors with soft, or all muted colors. The folding is easy and the possibilities are endless.

THE PAPER

Patterned chiyogami papers are a feature of the Japanese doll festival known as Kamibina. These high-quality papers are silkscreened by hand with lovely designs reminiscent of kimono fabric patterns in rich and lively pigment-dyed colors. This inkwell card showcases the decorative surface of this colorful paper, which, like the other Japanese papers, folds well and adheres neatly. This inkwell is so decorative you might not want to keep it hidden within an envelope. You can instead make it into a brooch, which can be pinned to the front of a card and then removed later to be worn by the card recipient. Simply mount the inkwell on heavy cardstock, cut it out carefully, and glue a brooch finding to the back.

Cherryl Moote

1. Cut a 4") square of very light weight paper such as chiyogami or origami paper. Fold the square diagonally in both directions. Unfold.

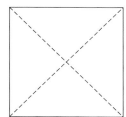

2. With the good side of the paper down, fold the corners to the center.

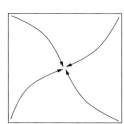

3. Turn the paper over keeping it on the point. Fold the left, top, and right sides to the middle.

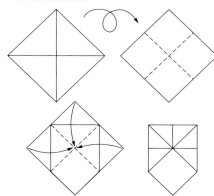

4. Turn the paper over again. Keep the pointed sections to the bottom. Fold the top left and top right corners to the center.

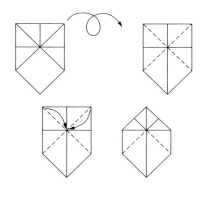

5. Turn the paper over again. Find the pointed flap of paper in the center.

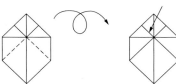

Pull the flap of paper up while pushing the top and bottom of the slit together and flatten it to form the mouth of the inkwell. Another way to think of this is to squeeze open the mouth by pushing on the top and bottom of the opening.

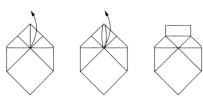

6. Leaving the mouth of the inkwell intact, unfold the sides back to the way they looked in Step 3. First you unfold the left and right top diagonal edges by finding the points at the center back and bringing them towards the front.

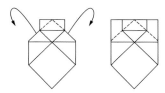

Then you unfold the flaps that are in the center at the front. Remember to keep the mouth of the inkwell intact.

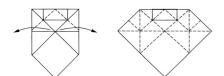

7. Fold the left and right edges to the back as shown. This will form the shoulders of the inkwell.

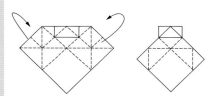

8. Fold the bottom of the inkwell up and to the back.

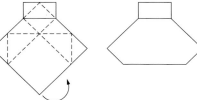

Instructions by Cherryl Moote

DECORATIVE PHOTO CORNERS

*W*ith a simple origami technique known as a kite fold, you can turn small pieces of solid or patterned scrap paper into decorative photo corners for the featured photo on your scrapbook page. Choose papers with contrasting or complementary colors and patterns—or look for inspiration in the colors and patterns within the photograph itself.

Creating the Project

1 Make each photo corner from a small square of paper. The size of the square depends on the size of your photo. For a standard-size photo (4 x 6 inches), work with 1 ½-inch squares.

Experiment to find the size you like best. Follow the instructions on the opposite page to make the folded paper corners. Add them to the corners of your photograph before mounting the photo to your mat or scrapbook page. Add a bit of adhesive behind each photo mount, too.

2 Cut nine tear-drop shapes and three circles from colored paper and place them on the background sheet.

3 Cut two mats from colored paper. The first, striped, mat (on which we are mounting the photograph, with its corners) is larger than the photograph—approximately ¼ inch larger on all four sides—and the pink one is ¼ inch larger than the striped one. Mount the mats on the page and add the stitching detail. Add the four corners to the photograph and mount on the striped mat.

Making Folded Paper Corners

1. Start with a square of paper.

2. Fold up, and crease.

3. Open flat, fold down, and crease.

4. Open flat and turn paper over.

5. Bring corners together as shown, forming a triangle, and crease.

6. Open flat, fold, and crease in the opposite direction.

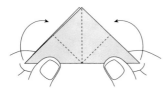 

7. (a) Holding folded corners in either hand, push fingers toward center, forming a pocket opening,

(b) then move the corner in your left hand to the back and the one in your right hand to the front, forming a layered triangle as shown.

8. Bring top right flap perpendicular to center fold.

9. Use a pencil, narrow object, or craft knife to open the edges of raised flap.

10. Keeping center creases aligned, press flat, creasing both sides of the new kite shape. Turn paper over and repeat.

FOLDED FRAME

*F*olded papers make dramatic, decorative frames for your favorite photographs. This folded frame is easy to make and adds a three-dimensional effect to any card front or scrapbook page. You can work with a double-sided patterned paper to add more variety and color to the design. The side that is facing up when you begin the folding sequence will be the side that frames your photograph.

Creating the Project

1. Crop three or more photos to their finished size. Vary the sizes to add interest to the page.

2. Cut a square of double-sided patterned paper for each of the photographs. The squares should be at least ¾ inch larger than the photo on each side. Follow the drawing and instructions, opposite, to fold the frames. Arrange the mounts on the page, glue them in place, and tuck the photos inside.

3. Glue a few strands of ribbon "stems" to the flowers. Pierce the paper and insert ribbon to tie a bow around the bouquet. Nestle the tips of two or more simple folded "leaf" shapes and attach them to the "stems"—just for fun.

Making Origami Paper Frames

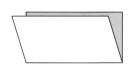

1. Start with a square of paper, printed side up.

2. Fold up, and crease.

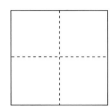

3. Open flat, fold over, and crease.

4. Open flat.

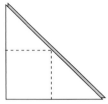

5. Make a diagonal fold, and crease.

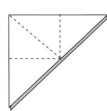

6. Open flat; make the opposite diagonal fold, and crease.

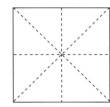

7. Open flat.

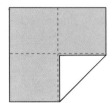

8. Fold one corner to the center point.

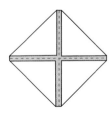

9. Continue to fold the other three points to the center. Rotate.

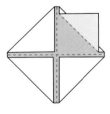

10. Fold one point out three-fourths of the way to its original fold. Crease.

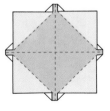

11. Fold and crease the other three points the same way.

12. Insert your photo beneath the frame and flatten.

ACCORDION BOOK

Accordion books are sometimes also called concertina books. You can create one simply by folding a long strip of paper to create a zigzag of pages. The finished book can be stored on a shelf, like any other bound book—or it can be displayed with the pages fanned open so the contents are on display. This design variation has a pocket along the bottom, where you can tuck ticket stubs, vintage postage stamps, or other small treasures.

Cherryl Moote

Creating the Project

1. Cut a sheet of medium-weight paper (lightweight enough that it does not need to be scored before folding) into a long strip, with the grain parallel to the height of the paper.

2. To create the pocket opening, which runs along the length of the strip, fold up the entire bottom edge to the finished depth you want.

3. To create the book pages, fold the strip in half widthwise and open it again. Fold one end of the strip to the center and fold the other end to meet it. Open the strip. Now fold it into an accordion by alternating the direction of the folds. Check that all folds match precisely.

4. Continue to fold each section in half, making sure that your folds are accurate. Repeat the process until the pages are the width you desire.

5. Tuck items into each of the pockets. Add ribbons or fiber pulls to add texture and interest.

EXTENDED WISHES

You can turn simple white cardstock into a creative and surprising multilayered message—and a showcase of your favorite materials and techniques. Don't forget to include journaling—the most important way to share your heartfelt feelings. Unify the pages into a harmonious design by maintaining a simple color scheme through-out. The soft greens and purples of this charming accordion card (made with a purhcased accordion book) recall the seasonal shades of the springtime holiday.

This designer filled the sleeves with her own memorabilia. One can always make such a book by hand, but you don't have to. There are plenty of wonderful products available commerically. Don't hesitate to use them.

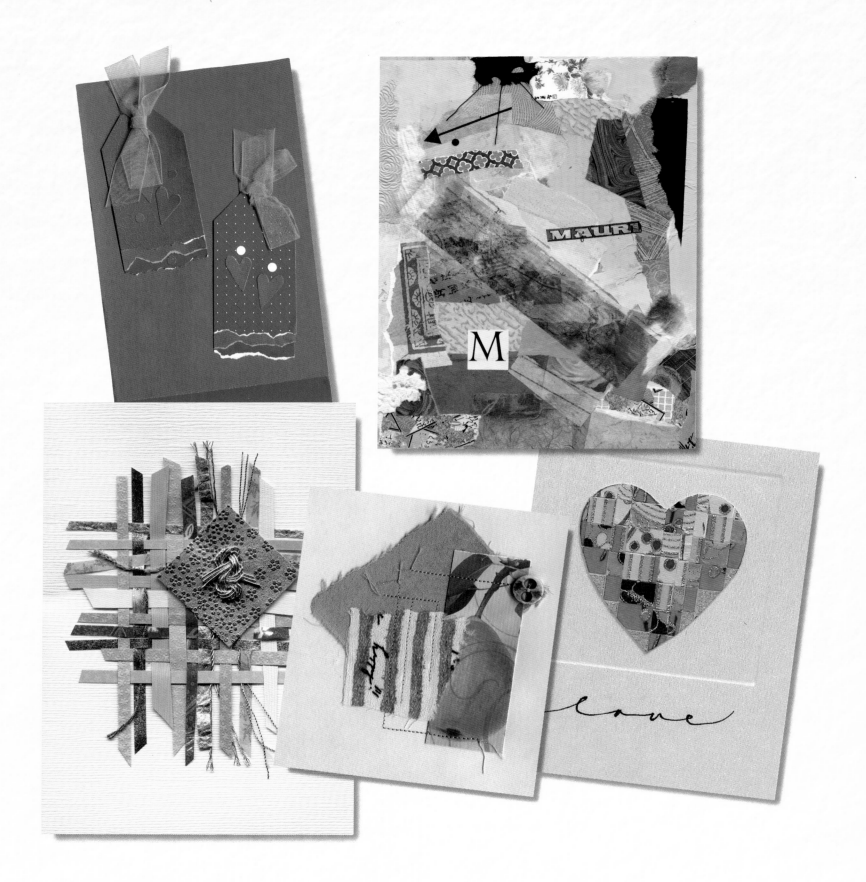

COLLAGE

*T*he craft of paper collage has existed for centuries in the folk art of cultures around the world. Many twentieth-century artists—such as Picasso and Matisse—also created paper collages.

In paper collage, you arrange different sizes, colors, and types of paper—photographs, newsprint, specialty papers, scrap papers—to form a pleasing composition. You can also integrate fabric, metal, and wooden objects to add texture and interest. When you have decided on the best arrangement, simply glue your materials to a solid, stamped, painted, or patterned paper surface. By combining techniques and materials, you can create geometric or random patterns or abstract images and designs. You can also create pictures, scenes, still lifes, and portraits by carefully planning and positioning the pieces.

Paper collage provides the perfect opportunity to play with color, shape, and texture. A collage can contain any type of paper—packaged coordinated papers, handmade novelty sheets, newsprint, old letters, postcards, cancelled stamps, candy wrappers, bus and theater tickets, paper bags, aluminum foil, gift wrap, you name it. Be on the lookout for colorful, intriguing, or personally meaningful recycled papers that you can transform into a collage.

Don't hesitate to add punch art, rubber stamping, stickers, and other paper craft techniques to your collage, too. Draw or paint finishing touches and small details with acrylics, watercolors, colored pens, pencils, or markers. Try working with wire, buttons, yarns, raffia, mizuhiki, metal charms, or other three-dimensional embellishments. In collage, everything goes!

STAR CARD

*T*orn paper has a soft, natural edge that reveals the structure of the paper. Combine cut shapes, which have straight edges, with torn shapes, which have ragged edges, to create contrast, texture, and interest. The angled edges of this tag contrast with two layers of soft torn edges. The intersecting horizontal and vertical lines of the mesh contrast with the narrow strip of torn paper laid across its surface. The bow tied with a strand of glistening fiber, a faux-stitched (with markers) pop-up star, and a central decorative brad add extra interest and dimension.

Petite Motifs

Petite Motifs

NOTE OF THANKS

*T*his note card combines circles, circle patterns, straight lines, and torn edges. The round, red mat is enhanced by the addition of round, red brads. Round, red dots pepper the background of the paper pattern, too. The red brads secure a strip of torn vellum on top of two strips of torn patterned paper. The torn textures are neatly contained within a shipping-tag shape and are accented with button brads above and below and a fringe of colorful fiber strands.

HEART TAGS

hese punched hearts dance on multiple layers of patterned-paper tags—their precise shapes contrasting with the soft, undulating torn edges. Torn colored paper often has a white edge, which itself can create an interesting effect. To control the amount of white you reveal, tear toward or away from the right side of the paper. The side you tear toward will have more white surface exposed. The sheer-ribbon bows tied at the top of the tags have a golden sheen that echoes the shimmer of the antique-gold papers.

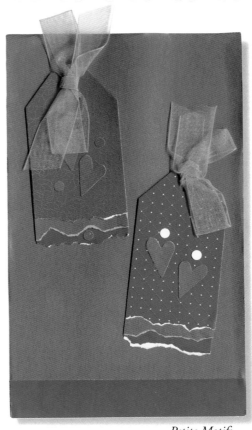

Petite Motifs

Petite Motifs

HEART CARD

o make this clever yet simple card, a strip of robin's-egg paper is torn against the grain along both edges to create a rough-textured edge. The strip is placed across the "seam" of two straight-edge sweetheart-red textured papers. The effect fools the eye! You think you are seeing torn edges on the pink papers and a robin's-egg background between them. Die-cut hearts of glitter paper are topped with sheer pink ribbons to complete the composition.

SPARKLING HEART

Collage invites you to play with surfaces, color, and texture. This glistening note card is a showcase of smooth and textured metallic surfaces. The many narrow strips that make up the heart are cut in varying lengths from decorative papers. The strips are laid precisely side by side to fill the hand-cut heart shape, and occasionally alternate with rows of tiny metallic beads, mizuhiki, or strands of silver and gold metallic threads. The background sheet is subtly flecked with metallic paint, and a silver-mesh bow adds a sparkling finishing touch.

Geney Levin

COLLAGE STRIP CARD

When creating a shape or background, you can lay strips of paper—of the same or varying widths—side by side or you can weave them together to create more-intricate texture. To make this note card, the artist cut cardstock and paper of various colors and textures into strips of approximately equal lengths. Some ends were slightly angled to add more interest and movement to the design. She wove the strips together in an alternating over-and-under pattern, and occasionally wove in strands of fiber.

The center medallion is a small square of gold paper stamped with a scattered plum stamp and embossed with gold metallic ink. Three short lengths of mizuhiki cord were tied to form a decorative knot. Mizuhiki is traditionally used in Japan to tie and decorate gift packages.

Sally Traidman

84

SUNBURST

This cheerful canvas is made up of three mini canvases. Each has its own background and color scheme—and each is a satisfying composition in and of itself. The canvas is divided in half horizontally with a narrow striped strip, whose colors harmonize with the blue field on one side of it and complement the orange field on the other. One half is also divided vertically—and asymmetrically—with color blocking. Each of the three mini canvases features its own centerpiece: an intriguing foreign postage stamp, a quadrant of small black-and-white stamped spiral suns, and a punched, layered—and popped—blazing-sunlike floral motif.

Geney Levin

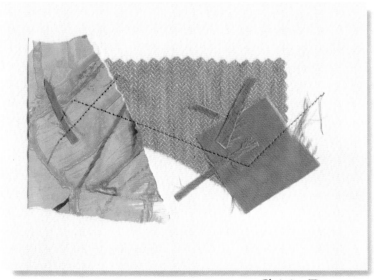

Christine Timmons

COLLAGE CARDS

Paper pieces are straight-cut and torn. The fabrics are pinked and raveling. Geometric lines of machine stitching draw the eye across the canvas and add texture, color, and a bit of sparkle. The button? An unexpected and perfect surprise. The stitches on the underside are not concealed. This artist prefers to "celebrate the stitches," either leaving them as is or decorating around them with colored pencil, ink, or paint.

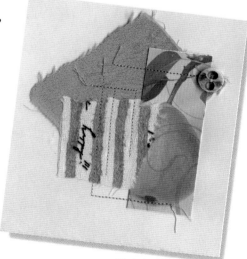

Christine Timmons

BARGELLO

*B*argello is a style of needlepoint that originated in Florence, Italy, in the seventeenth century. It was used to create wool upholstery fabrics and wall hangings. The style is characterized by a geometric pattern and a type of zigzag flame stitch with a rhythmic rise and fall of "flames" of color. Both quilters and paper crafters have adapted bargello to their own materials. The technique makes wonderful central designs for scrapbook pages, greeting cards, gift tags, and framed artwork. This project was created from Magenta's Bargello Paper Quilting Kit. The artwork was designed and created by Nathalie Métivier.

Creating the Project

1 Stamp and decorate six 8-inch-long strips of paper of equal widths.

2 Peel off the liner on one side of the adhesive sheet. Working from the top edge of the sheet, lay the strips close together, making sure their ends are aligned. Press firmly on the strips to adhere them well. Cut around the edges of the rectangle, removing any extra adhesive.

3 Lay a transparent quilt ruler on top of the rectangle. With a craft knife, cut across the ends of the horizontal strips to create 11 new, multicolored, vertical strips of varying widths. Position the vertical strips on a piece of cardstock that is the finished dimension of your artwork. Remove the liner on the back of the first strip, and align one end with the top left-hand edge of the cardstock. Lay each of the next five strips, each time staggering their placement by one color block.

4 Cut the extra pieces from the bottom of each staggered strip and add the piece to the top of the cardstock to complete the row.

5 Position the remaining strips to create a symmetrical color pattern with the first half of the design. You can bring the deep V of the pattern all the way to the bottom of the artwork or you could reverse it at any point you choose.

Nathalie Métivier

GIFT CARD

*B*argello can stand on its own, as in the previous example, or it can be used to create shapes suited to more specific greetings. The rotating card technique lets you showcase interesting papers and your paper-engineering skills. The stunning card is simple to make. With the card closed, draw a light pencil line down the center of the card. (You'll erase it later.) Open the card and cut three sides of a rectangular shape from the center line to the left, leaving the right side attached to the center line of the card. Score the center pencil line above and below the rectangle and fold the front of the card to the left on the score line (bring the right front edge to the fold at the left), allowing the cut portion of the rectangle to swing inside the card. Add your art-work. In this project, the designer wrapped the bargello gift with a charming ribbon.

Cherryl Moote

BARGELLO HEART

*U*sing the same papers as the Gift Card above, the designer created a wonderfully different effect. A die-cut or punched heart shape frames the artwork, creating a bargello heart within a distinctive dry-embossed recessed square—a perfect presentation for an elegant card for a special moment. The simple script message is a lovely addition.

Cherryl Moote

MOSAIC

Simply by cutting paper, you can quickly and easily create dramatic mosaics to feature as a central design on a note card or as a piece of artwork. Mosaic patterns also make wonderful borders and frames.

Stamp or paint an overall design on a square or rectangle of paper or cardstock. Or work with a decorative paper that has a bold overall pattern.

With a straightedge and pencil, divide the square into a grid of horizontal and vertical lines. Cut the small squares with a craft knife and reassemble them on a contrasting background paper or cardstock, leaving a small amount of equal space around and between each one. The reassembled design will create one decorative pattern; the grid of space between the squares will create another.

Nathalie Métivier

Experiment with photographs to create some wonderful mosaic effects. For more abstract variations, rearrange the squares before you reassemble them—the original image will no longer be recognizable, but new and exciting patterns will emerge.

GEISHA'S KIMONO

*W*hen thinking about collage, consider the same principles of design that you would when creating any other piece of artwork or when designing a scrapbook page: balance, contrast, focus, color, proportion, texture, pattern, and harmony. Think about the purpose of the piece you are making—or the impression or feeling you'd like to convey. Choose papers with colors and patterns that work well together, remembering that you will also want to add accents with contrasting but harmonious colors.

Japanese patterned papers and calligraphy form the background for this multilayered collage. They also support the theme of the geisha's traditional costume. The Yusen paper also recalls the ancient tradition of collage. Foreign coins and currency represent the costly measures that were required to produce the beautiful and colorful traditional garment. Joss paper expresses respect for the geisha tradition, and the insect motifs symbolize her graceful movements during the many ceremonies she performed. The three-dimensional objects create a sense of weight and permanence, to represent the lasting tradition of the geisha and the many heavy layers of the kimono itself. The artist also worked with rubber-stamped designs, a metal-rimmed tag, charms, golden gel medium, and white gesso to create the design.

Kayce Carey

CIGAR BOX CLUTCH

Collage can be as simple as gluing a few strips of paper to form a flat composition—or as complex as constructing a large, intricate sculpture. Collage artists often combine many different types of materials—paper, paint, metal, and wood, fiber, and other natural materials—to create mixed-media pieces. (The technique of adding objects to paper collage is sometimes called assemblage.) This artist embellished a wooden cigar box to create a decorative commentary on money—the reason to carry a purse in the first place. The box is covered with foreign currency (decoupage-style), foreign coins, and other metal pieces. The purse's decorative scroll handle is actually an old metal drawer pull. Foil, Gildenglitz, and luminescent acrylic paints applied to the coins, the surface of the purse, and the handle add a touch of glitter and glamour.

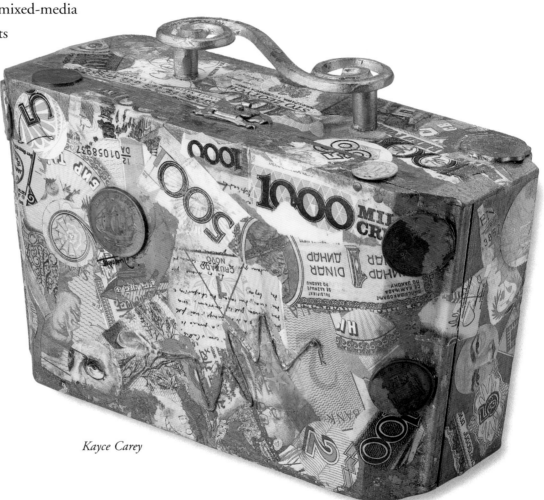

Kayce Carey

PARIS COUTURE

*T*ear a variety of papers into different sizes and shapes. Organize them by pattern and color to make it easy to make selections as you work. You can create your collage on a solid, colored, painted, or stamped background or you can cover the entire surface. The pastel colors of the many layers of paper in this collage—including mulberry, onion, and banana fiber—create the feeling of a Paris runway in spring, during the unveiling of the season's newest fashions. The pink, yellow, and green shades are unified with neutral white and cream shades. The photographic images and printed elements support the theme and ground the fibrous white-onion-paper foundation. Dress-pattern tissue, an antique button card, golden gel medium, and white gesso add even more interest and texture to the composition.

Kayce Carey

TIME TRAVEL

*B*old primary colors, in various patterns and textures, add a new dimension to this view of time and space. Rich orange and gold Japanese Joss and Yusen papers create a sense of dynamic movement within the design. The artist chose bold green and yellow textures to create a feeling of fantasy and joy. She chose red to create excitement and focus. The torn black papers anchor the other colors, stabilizing them in space. The printed elements create movement and guide the viewer's eye across the canvas.

Kayce Carey

BEADED CARD

The centerpiece of this composition is a folded strip of a double-woven fabric—the pattern appears on both sides of the fabric, although the colors alternate. The bottom edge of the strip is snipped to form a raveling and jagged edge. Then the strip is folded and secured by hand with pink rayon embroidery thread and random stitches. Knots and beads are scattered along the surface of the card to add more texture and dimension. This artist makes her note cards with printmaking paper (available at art-supply stores). For clean edges, she cuts the cards with a craft knife and straightedge. For feathered edges, she simply tears the card to size, using a heavy metal ruler as a guide. She presses and sets the center fold with a bone folder.

Christine Timmons

Christine Timmons

BLACK AND BLUE CARD

This collage combines scraps of fabric, a photographic remnant from a quilt-show announcement, a triangular piece of mesh, and whole and halved felted self-adhesive rings—which mirror the dots in the fabric and the rings in the photograph. After gluing the elements in place, the artist sewed a zigzag line across a portion of the surface with a shiny pink rayon embroidery thread. Hand- or machine-sewn lines can randomly roam the card or can echo a shape or line in the fabric or paper elements.

SPECIAL EFFECTS

There are so many specialty techniques to help you create one-of-a-kind paper crafts. We have presented many throughout the book and are featuring a few more here, but we hope you'll never stop hunting for new possibilities. Many other crafts—particularly the fiber crafts, such as quilting, weaving, and embroidery—offer plenty of design inspiration and an array of techniques that can be easily adapted to paper.

You can also create dazzling special effects just by adding surprising, decorative embellishments to even the simplest design. Choose from a universe of likely and unlikely sources—from store-bought specialty items made for crafters to all the treasures you can find in hardware stores, fabric stores, stationery stores, or in the natural world around you. Consider sequins, pressed flowers, metal charms, seashells, buttons, beads, glitter glue, chalk, paper doilies, wire, wooly yarns, lace, raffia, jute, flower seeds, pins, ribbons, coins, and tassels—to name a few! The most ordinary item can turn a paper-craft project into an extraordinary work of art. There are no limits!

PAPER WEAVING

$\mathcal{P}$aper crafters can learn a lot from fabric artists. Many of the same techniques are effective with both types of materials. One of the simplest and most basic fabric techniques for paper crafters is paper weaving. By interlacing strips of paper of contrasting or complementary colors, textures, or patterns, you can create the illusion of rich woven fabrics. You can vary the effects to create everything from a knobby "handwoven" to a smooth-finished "satin." This project is made using Magenta's Coffe Table Books Kit

1 We have chosen a rich selection of colored papers to coordinate with the soft greens of the scrapbook album cover.

2 With a ruler and a craft knife, cut 4 strips of turquoise paper ¼ inch wide and the full length of the paper. Next cut 2 strips of purple, 3 strips of yellow, and 3 strips of blue paper. These 12 strips of paper will be woven in and out through the mesh that

covers the window in the album cover. Stamp the ornament onto the silver metallic foil disc sticker. Cut a circle slightly larger than the foil disc out of yellow cardstock as a mat. Cut the mesh piece to fit the back of the window, leaving enough mesh extending beyond the window to anchor it. Cut the blue paper to form a curtain over the back side of the mesh-covered window, leaving enough overhang to anchor the paper.

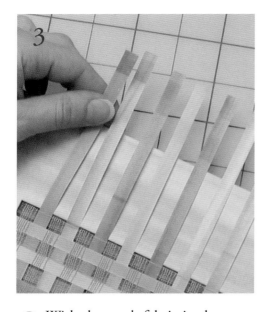

3 With the mesh fabric in the window, lay 5 strips of paper across the cover (we used a pattern of turquoise, yellow, blue, yellow, turquoise for the horizontal strips, and a pattern of turquoise, purple, blue, yellow, blue, purple, turquoise for the vertical strips). Weaving the horizontal strips in and out of the mesh,

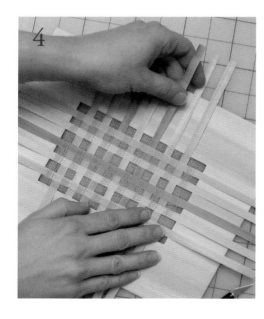

following the spacing of the woven pattern of the mesh. Repeat with the vertical strips.

4 Remove the backing paper from the silver foil sticker and affix it to the yellow mat. Attach the matted discs to the mesh widow. Cover the back of the mesh window with colored paper. As a decorative accent, paint the stamped foil sticker.

Nathalie Métivier

PIERCED PAPER

*B*y piercing small holes in paper, you can also add a lacy, delicate texture or pattern to borders, frames, mats, and large background areas. Your designs can be as simple or as complex as you please, but the look is always charming and sophisticated. You can also combine paper piercing with many other techniques—such as embossing, stippling, stamping, and painting.

These two elegant note cards were made by piercing the outline of a simple design—to showcase a simple message stamped with metallic ink. The "Thank You" card was pierced from front to back. The "Peace" card was pierced from back to front.

RIGHT OR WRONG

To make this card, place your stencil on the right or wrong side of the card, depending on the finished effect you want. Piercing on the right side will leave smooth hole openings on the front of the card. Piercing on the wrong side will leave raised holes. Working on a foam mat, piercing pad, or other padded surface, insert the needle tool through each hole to create the design. When you have finished, hold the design up to the light to make sure you have not skipped any of the holes. Stamp your message with metallic or colored ink.

PIERCED PAPER PLUS

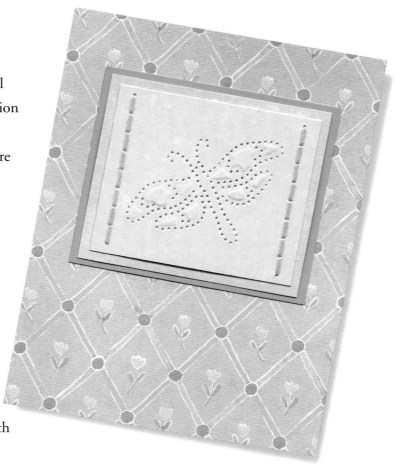

*D*ry embossing is the perfect complement to paper piercing. Dry embossing, also known as pressure embossing, creates a beautiful effect in parchment, vellum, and other types of paper—adding dimension and texture. The technique is most effective on light-colored or white papers, which show the outlines and shadows of the raised surfaces more clearly, as in the wings of this dragonfly/butterfly.

Creating the Project

1. With low-tack masking tape, attach a dragonfly stencil to the right side of a piece of bright-colored paper or cardstock.

2. Working on a foam pad or piercing pad, outline the dragonfly with a fine piercing tool. Hold the tool perpendicular to the surface of the paper, with your fingers close to the nib for better control, so the holes will be straight and even.

3. Turn the paper over on the foam pad. Trace the outlines of the small areas within the wings, then emboss them by rubbing firmly with a stylus tool.

4. Lay a stitching template on the front of the paper and pierce a row of evenly spaced holes on either side of the butterfly design. Trim the paper to the finished size you want for the note card.

5. With an embroidery needle, stitch embroidery floss through one row of holes, working in back stitch from the wrong side of the paper. Tape the thread ends to the wrong side of the paper. Stitch the second row and tape the thread ends.

6. Mount the design on two squares of complementary-colored papers. Then mount the squares onto the front of your note card.

TIP

*E*ven piercing—with holes of equal size placed at an even distance from each other—is the best technique to use when outlining a shape.

INTRICATE COMBINATIONS

$\mathcal{T}$his matching set of baby announcements, thank-you notes, and gift cards from Ecstasy Crafts combines the techniques of embroidery on paper, paper piercing, and incire paper cutting. Incire is a method of creating special effects by cutting patterns in paper and then folding parts of the design back onto itself. The soft-pastel color scheme, the translucent vellum, satiny ribbons, and tiny glistening beads make these delightful items a wonderful welcome to a new baby.

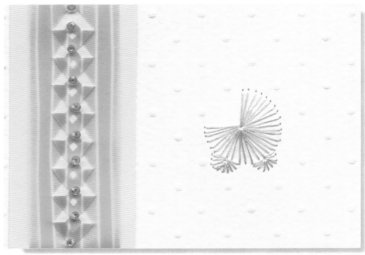

Marilynne Oskamp

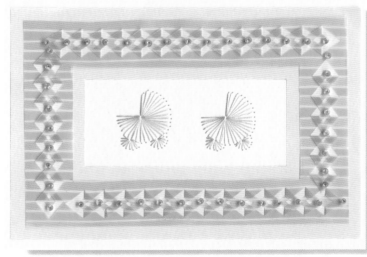

Marilynne Oskamp

Creating the Project

1. Working with a background stencil, emboss one half of the front of the card with polka dots.

2. Cut a 1-inch by 3½-inch strip of striped vellum. Cut a strip of lightweight pink cardstock to the same size.

3. Center the vellum strip on top of the incire template. (Position it over the second pattern in from the right, triangle points up.) Fold a small amount of vellum over the top of the card and position the first triangle close to the fold. Cut eight triangles with a craft knife.

4. Score the bottom edges of the triangles with the tip of the incire folding tool or a small ball embossing tool. Working from the bottom, fold down the top of each triangle.

5. Adhere the vellum design on top of the pink strip. With a very fine piercing tool, pierce small holes just below the tip of each folded triangle, piercing through the vellum and the cardstock.

6. Sew the vellum to the card, threading pink beads onto the needle as you stitch. Tape the ends of the thread to the back. Fold the edges of the vellum and pink strips to the inside of the card front and tape in place.

7. Pierce the pattern for the baby carriage in the center of the polka-dotted area. Embroider with a double strand of pink rayon thread, always working through the center holes. Tape the ends to the inside of the card front. Finish the card by lining with cream-colored cardstock.

Marilynne Oskamp

The stunning incire frames, opposite, are intriguing. The background paper visible in the incire border enhances the design. If you use paper with a different color on each side, on top of a third color background paper, you have a three-color design.

Creating the Project

1. Pierce the outside edge of a pink bib card, working with the provided Pattern A. With a white gel pen, trace the scalloped edge of Pattern B onto striped vellum.

2. Perforate around each scallop with a 2-needle split tool. (Place one of the needles in a pierced hole each time you pierce so that all the holes are evenly spaced.) When you have finished, gently press your thumbnail close the edge of the vellum to remove the excess. Emboss a small flower into each scallop.

3. With a white gel pen, trace the scalloped edge of Pattern C onto vellum. Perforate around each scallop with the 2-needle split tool and gently press out.

4. From the back, perforate each scallop a flower tool. Perforate three more flower motifs across the front of the small vellum bib. Emboss small designs with the star embossing tool at the inner point of each scallop. Emboss four more stars between the flowers on the front of the bib. Place a small pink dot into the center of each star.

5. Photocopy the baby carriage pattern. Center the photocopy on the vellum bib and pierce with fine and coarse piercing tools. Embroider with a fine needle and a knotted double strand of pink embroidery floss or rayon machine-embroidery thread. Always work through the center holes. Secure the thread at start and finish by tying a small knot at the back of the vellum. Cut the tail end close to the knot.

6. Attach all the bib layers by gluing the shoulder areas with a silicon-based glue. Glue a small pink bow at each shoulder.

SPIRELLI AND EMBROIDERED FLOWERS

*S*pirelli, also known as string art, is a fast and fun way to embellish handmade greeting cards, scrapbook pages, or the pages of an altered book. The linear geometric patterns are dazzling, and by combining different colored threads, you can work even the simplest design in a hundred variations. Not all spirelli effects have to be circular. You can create triangular and oval shapes, quasars, and combinations of all of these, too. These projects were created by Marilynne Oskamp for Ecstasy Crafts.

Marilynne Oskamp

TIP

*Y*ou can also emboss a pattern on the right side of the paper to create a concave effect, which will have deeper shadows and shading. This technique is called debossing.

Creating the Project

1. Emboss the corners of a 4½-inch square cardstock. Working on a foam pad, cut out enclosed areas with a craft knife.

2. Center the circle of flowers pattern on the square. Pierce the design with very fine and coarse piercing tools.

3. Embroider the flowers with red and dark yellow thread, always working through the center hole of the motif. Embroider the leaves with dark green thread. Secure thread ends at the back.

4. Attach the embossed and embroidered square to a square note card. Punch a medium spirelli flower in dark cardstock.

5. Tape one end of dark yellow thread to the back of the spirelli flower. Start the thread between any two petals and skip 10 petals before wrapping the thread around the flower. Continue wrapping, working clockwise, maintaining the interval of 10 petals. When you have returned to the starting point, tape the end of the petals.

6. Next, wrap a dark green thread around the flower, skipping seven petals. Then wrap a double strand of red thread, skipping seven petals.

7. Attach the flower to the note card with foam-mounting tape, centering it in the circle of embroidered flowers. Add a small gold sticker dot to the tip of each petal.

Creating the Project

1. Punch a medium spirelli flower in dark cardstock. Cut the cardstock into the shape of a gift tag. Cut a slightly larger gift tag in a light-colored cardstock. Cut a third gift tag, slightly larger than the light tag, in dark cardstock. Attach the small dark tag to the light tag.

2. Pierce tiny holes in each corner of the light tag. Stitch a single strand of red thread around the tag to form a frame. Tape the ends of the thread to the back of the tag at start and finish.

3. Punch a small spirelli flower in dark cardstock. Tape one end of a dark green thread to the back of the flower. Start the thread between any two petals and skip nine petals before wrapping the thread around the flower. Continue wrapping, working clockwise, maintaining the interval of nine petals. At the starting point, tape the end of the thread to the back of the flower.

4. Next, wrap dark yellow thread around the flower, skipping seven petals. Then wrap a red thread, skipping six petals.

5. Attach the spirelli flower to the tag with foam-mounting tape, centering it in the punched frame. Attach the light tag to the large dark tag. Add small gold sticker dots inside the petals of the frame.

6. Punch through all the layers to create a hole at the top of the tag. Place a gold flower sticker around the punched hole on the front and back of the tag. You can also thread a gold ribbon through the hole as a decorative pull.

Die-cut designs are available in a variety of shapes and sizes. This card was made using the small spirelli flower punch. The dark blue against the white cardstock offers a dramatic presentation.

Marilynne Oskamp

Marilynne Oskamp

GEOMETRY MAGENTA STYLE

*T*his intricate, pieced floral motif takes its inspiration from the classic designs found on ornate Mediterranean tile mosaics. The decorative pattern is created by stamping sheets of self-adhesive plainstock with three basic geometric shapes: squares, diamonds, and triangles. The quiltlike pattern is formed by cutting out the shapes (before the lining is removed) and then arranging the different-shaped stickers according to the pattern. You can also create this design by stamping paper or cardstock and adhering the pieces to double-sided clear adhesive. This project was created using Magenta's Kit.

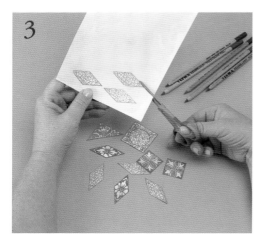

Creating the Project

1 Color two to three sheets of 8 ½ x 11-inch self-adhesive plainstock with pigment Cat's Eye. Color each sheet with a different light-colored pigment and a direct-to-paper technique.

2 Stamp the colored plainstock with geometric stamps in multiple

sizes. Work with a dark permanent ink. Stamp the images so that they are close together to use the entire sheet efficiently. The size of your design will determine how many images you need to stamp. Enhance the stamped images with colored pencils.

3 Cut out the geometric images with scissors or a craft knife, using a ruler as a guide. Be sure your cuts are

precise as they will affect how well the pieces fit together.

4 Remove the paper backing and arrange the geometric shapes. (Plainstock can be repositioned after the backing is removed.) Position the shapes according to the pattern with light pressure. Play with the placement until you are satisfied with the arrangement. When you have the design as you want it, apply heavier pressure.

5 Trim the design to even any irregular edges. Mount the artwork on a 12-inch square of dark-colored cardstock. Hide any gaps or creative flaws in the design with metallic-ink markers or colored pencils.

Nathalie Métivier

QUILTING

Quilters can certainly teach paper crafters a thing or two. Quilts are made of geometric shapes cut and sewn from fabric—but you can assemble the same decorative patterns by cutting and gluing photographs and papers. Colorful backgrounds, collages, and mats can be arranged in patchwork, Log Cabin, Lone Star, or Tumbling Block patterns. Browse through quilt pattern books for more ideas and inspiration.

Nathalie Métivier

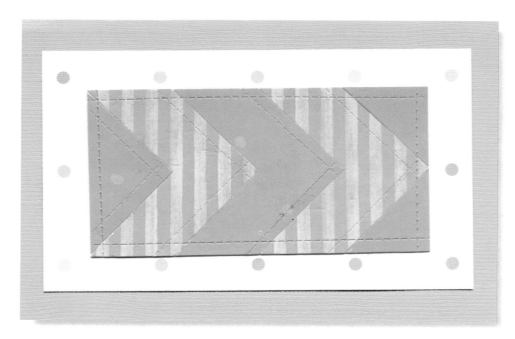

The traditional Log Cabin quilt block design works beautifully as a pieced cover design for a small book. Cut the paper strips from complementary and contrasting patterned and solid papers. Add fiber decorative elements to embellish the cover.

A chevron punch created the Flying Geese quilt pattern, which is completed with perforated faux stitching. The various color polka dots surrounding the image extend the sunny palette.

he Tumbling Block quilt pattern lends itself beautifully to a series of close-up photos. Two patterned papers form the sides of the blocks. Delightful die-cut flowers and a flower pot embellish the page.

PAPER SPIRALS

*L*ong quilled paper spirals can resemble lines of stitching within a "quilted" design or work as a decorative, three-dimensional outline for specific shapes within pictorial designs, as for this colorful schoolhouse. Spirals are also sometimes known as ropes or twists.

Simply wind a thin, colored strip of paper—about ⅛ to ¾ inch wide—around the tool. You can work with quilling needles, knitting needles, a wooden skewer, or even a toothpick. Coil the strand diagonally along the length of the tool to form the spiral. Press the spiral firmly against the tool with your fingers to "set" the shape. Attach one end of the spiral to the page with a drop of glue so the spiral will not unwind.

TIP

*T*he long spirals frame the schoolhouse. The small sprials double as a garden of little pencils and crayons for the kindergarteners.

Pam Klassen

QUILLING

*Q*uilling—also known as paper filigree or scroll work—is the art of rolling narrow strips of paper into coiled shapes and combining the shapes to form decorative designs. Filigree was popular among fashionable women in England during the eighteenth century. They used quilling to decorate tea caddies, work baskets, cribbage boards, and even furniture. The Colonists coined the term "quilling" and decorated boxes, trays, and other everyday items. In these projects, quilling holds center stage, as the featured artwork on note cards—suitable for framing or displaying.

" Friendship is the gold thread that ties hearts together."

Sherry Crocker

Basic Quilled Shapes

LOOSE GLUED COIL

Roll the paper on the quilling tool to form a coil. Remove the coil from the tool. Allow the coil to relax and expand to desired size, and apply small amount of glue to the end of paper strip, gluing down to the coil.

TIGHT COIL

Roll the paper on the quilling tool to form a coil. DO NOT allow the coil to relax and expand. While the coil is still on the tool, apply small amount of glue to the end of paper strip, gluing down to the coil. Gently remove the coil from tool.

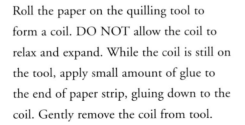

TEARDROP

Make a loose glued coil. Pinch at one end of the coil to form a teardrop shape.

SHAPED TEARDROP

Make a teardrop. Run your fingernail toward the point curling the point in one direction.

SQUARE

Make a loose glued coil. Flatten the coil between the fingers. Hold the flattened coil upright between thumb and index finger with the points at the top and bottom. Flatten again matching up the previous 2 folds created by the points. Reopen to form a square shape.

HALF CIRCLE

Make a loose glued coil. Flatten one side of the coil by pinching the circle at two points or flatten coil gently against finger.

Quilling Shapes and Instructions by Jan Williams

BRIDE'S HAT

*M*ake two tight coils of white quilling paper. With a small rounded object, or the pad of your finger, gently push the underside of the second coil, to form a dome. This shape is sometimes called a grape roll. Apply glue to the underside to keep the shape from collapsing. Glue the grape roll to the first (base) coil. Glue the ends of a 2-inch-long strip to form a loop. Pinch the loop at the center and secure to form a bow. Create streamers for the bow with a 2-inch strip of ⅛-inch white paper, folded in half. Tuck the folded center of the streamers under the bow and attach the ribbon to the bride's hat.

"I do."

"One penny, two penny, three penny, four: saving up for the ice cream store."

Sherry Crocker

"Feeling gratitude and not expressing it is like wrapping a present and not giving it."

William Arthur Ward

Sherry Crocker

Basic Quilled Shapes

TRIANGLE

Make a teardrop shape. Hold the teardrop at the pointed end between the thumb & index finger. Gently press the rounded end back until 3 points are formed.

BUNNY EAR

Make a loose glued coil. Gently push the coil against the quilling tool (1/4" diameter) to form a shape similar to the crescent, however with the 2 points closer together.

SHAPED MARQUISE

Make a marquise. Run your fingernail toward one point curling it up. Repeat at the other end curling in the opposite direction.

MARQUISE

Make a loose glued coil. Pinch at the exact opposite side of coil to form points at both ends, forming a marquise shape.

HOLLY LEAF

Make a loose glued coil. Flatten the coil between the fingers. Hold the flattened coil in the center tightly with tweezers. Gently push one end towards center with index finger & thumb forming 2 more points. Repeat on opposite end. Reshape leaf as needed.

OPEN HEART

Fold a piece of paper in half. Rolling towards the centerfold, roll each end of paper inward toward the centerfold.

ROLLED HEART (ARROW)

Make a teardrop. Hold the teardrop shape between the thumb and index finger of one hand. Gently push the center of rounded end back using the straight edge of the tweezers. Crease at both sides of the pushed-in end.

RECTANGLE

Make a loose glued coil. Flatten the coil between the fingers. Hold the flattened coil upright between thumb & index finger with points at the top & bottom. Slowly begin to flatten the coil once again moving the previous points slightly away from each other rather than matching them as in the square shape. Reopen to form a rectangle.

CRESCENT

Make a teardrop. Pinch one more point not quite opposite of the first point. Run your fingernail toward both points curling the points up or make a loose glued coil. Press coil against the rounded side of the quilling tool or finger to give the coil a crescent shape.

"V" SHAPE

Fold the paper in half. Curl each end of paper away from centerfold forming semi-tight coils at each end.

Quilling Shapes and Instructions by Jan Williams

QUILLED GOOSE EGG

*T*he artist first colored this egg with a pigment ink pad and a "direct-to-egg" technique. The entire peach-colored egg is then covered with cascading quilled bleeding-heart branches made with various hues of peach-colored papers, accented with green quilled leaves. Once the coiled quilled shapes are made they can be affixed to any surface that will hold glue. Don't limit their application to paper.

Jan Williams

Jan Williams

QUILLED DAISY CARD

*T*he centerpiece of this card is the trio of bright yellow daiseis, quilled with narrow strips of yellow and blue papers. The leaves are made with a green paper with gold gilded edges. To quill an oval, or marquise, for the petals, simply flatten a loose coil between your thumb and forefinger to form a point at each end. To create the flame-shaped petals of the bending blossoms, form a teardrop and bend a pinched end slightly to one side.

QUILLED ROSES BOUQUET

*T*his card is made by twice folding a 15 x 6 1/2-inch piece of cardstock to form a 5 x 6 1/2-inch card with two inside pages. The quilling is made on the first inside page, and the lavish bouquet spills out of a window cut in the center of the card cover. The window is framed with mauve and green borders and defined by a thin gold rule. The quilled ecru and mauve roses are guilded with gold edges. The leaves are punched. The roses are folded and rolled with a slotted quilling tool. The slot holds the end of the paper securely and maintains even tension as you create each rose.

Jan Williams

Instructions for Quilling Roses

1. Hold the quilling tool perpendicular in the right hand. Thread the quilling paper onto tool from the left, with the paper horizontal to the tool. Roll the paper towards the left until you have made 1½ complete turns around the tool.

3. Start with a square of paper. Making the rest of your folds: Repeat the same instructions used for the first fold until you are at the end of your paper strip. Generally 3 inches of paper will yield 7-9 folds.

2. With the left hand, fold the paper down towards your body. The quilling paper should now be perpendicular against the tool, both going in the same direction. Hold the paper firmly in the left hand and rotate your right arm up while holding the tool to make the paper form a cone shape on the end of the tool. Bring your right arm back down keeping the "cone" shape.

4. Remove the folded rose from the tool. Hold the center of the rose with pointed tweezers and gently turn the paper outward, the opposite way you originally folded the paper. Gently fold the petals down by grabbing several layers of folds with the tweezers and pulling them down away from the center of the rose. Gently "smash" the rose between two fingers before gluing it in place.

Quilling Shapes and Instructions by Jan Williams

ALTERED BOOKS

*P*aper crafters have discovered a wonderful way to bring together their paper passions—between covers! Transform a damaged or discarded book into a multipage canvas to display a sampling of your favorite paper craft techniques. You can easily find old hardcover books of every shape and size at library sales, tag sales, or second-hand bookshops. Or rescue them from friends who are moving or cleaning house. Old books do not have to be tossed out!

You could turn a bound book into an actual scrapbook—just as people did in days gone by—to record memorable family events or personal history. Or you could make the book an original work of art in and of itself, with a specific theme or "plot." Or make each page entirely unique, changing themes and colors and materials as you progress through the pages. The choice is yours.

There are so many great things about crafting within the pages of a book. You have hundreds of pages to stamp, sticker, cut, paste, tie, stitch, paint, punch, and otherwise embellish. Incorporate some of your cherished mementos—photographs, concert tickets, favorite cards from friends, notes or ideas from your own journals. Not only will you finally get them out of hiding, you'll give them new meaning—and ensure their safekeeping! A bound book is a neat, compact, and durable way to keep three-dimensional and textured pages out of harm's way.

POCKET PAGES

The pages of an altered book can hold all sorts of treasures—precious mementos, inserted papers, or pull-out tags. Decide which objects you would like to include in each of the four pockets—metal-rimmed tags with photos, stamped tag stock, paper "money," and miniature "postcards" are just a few of the possibilities. Knowing in advance what you will place in each pocket helps you determine the depth of the pocket.

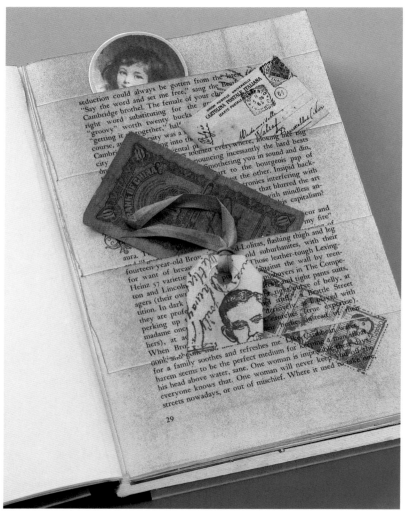

Kim Smith

Creating the Project

1. Cut four consecutive pages to graduated depths. Cut the first, shortest page first. The page strips can be any size. They don't have to be in even increments. These pages were cut to heights (starting from the bottom trim) of 2 inches, 4 inches, 6 inches, and 8 inches.

2. Color the surface of the layered pages by stippling or by working with a direct-to-paper technique.

3. On the reverse side of the first page, glue three sides (bottom, left, and right, leaving the top open) with double-sided tape or glue stick.

4. Tape three sides (leaving the top open) of the backs of the next three pages. Also apply horizontal strips of tape across one-half to three-quarters of the back surface, depending on the depth of the pocket.

5. Apply tape to the entire surface of the fifth (backing) page. Adhere it to the next page to add thickness and stability.

6. After all the pages are adhered—and before the items are placed in their pockets—stamp the stippled surface with an overall or random pattern.

Creating the Project

1. Fold four consecutive pages in your book to graduated widths. Fold the first page in thirds back to the spine. Fold the next page in half. Fold over one-quarter of the next page and about one-eighth of the next. Each page should extend beyond the previous page.

2. Glue each of the folded pages to itself, leaving a portion of the folds on the third and fourth pages free of adhesive to form a pocket.

3. Color both sides of each page with a direct-to-paper technique, varying the colors. (Put a piece of scrap paper between each page to protect it while you are working on the next.)

Kim Smith

4. Color the fifth consecutive page to create a full-page backing. Adhere the fifth page to the next page in the book to add thickness and stability—and to conceal any bleed-through.

5. Fold strips of ¼-inch-wide copper-foil tape or colored paper, cut them to length, and adhere them to the folded edges of each page.

6. Apply letter stickers to self-adhesive tiles to create your message or title. Stagger the placement of the tiles along the edges of the graduated pages—allowing half of each tile to overhang the fold. Rub the sticky backs of the tiles with powder to remove the adhesive on the overhang.

7. Make tags with a template and printed cardstock or with printed paper mounted on cardstock. Punch holes in the tags and attach decorative fiber pulls. Insert the tags in the pocket slots on the back of the third and fourth leaves.

GRADUATED POLKA DOT PAGES

*A*n altered book is an empty canvas—and there aren't many rules. Sometimes it's great fun to add an element of surprise by juxtaposing the serious theme of a book with a playful design. The pages of this volume of the *American People's Encyclopedia* have been spruced up with punched windows of bright color, a rainbow array of vibrant torn edges, and an edge-trimming of stamped metal-ringed tags.

Laurie Goodson

Creating the Project

1. Cut through the top third of nine consecutive pages. Tear the pages to graduated widths and apply bands of color to each torn edge.

2. Randomly punch holes in the remaining two-thirds of the first page. Add color to the page behind it so that color shows through the punched windows.

3. Glue all nine partial pages together.

4. Randomly punch a few holes in the facing page. Add color to the page behind it so that the color shows through the windows. Glue the page to a backing page.

5. Punch holes along the bottom or edge of the glued pages. Insert eyelets to hang colorful alphabet-stamped metal-rimmed tags or to attach a decorative edging. (If you are attaching tags, be sure you position the eyelets close enough to the edge of the paper so they hang freely—at least one-half the diameter of the ring.)

GARDEN PATH POCKET PAGE

*A*dd intrigue to your altered book by allowing the reader to explore and interact—by peeking through openings or reaching into pockets. Rather than folding pages to make side pockets, for this project you simply tear the pages at an angle to make a large top pocket. Attach a decorative edging, an unexpected detail or two—stamped images, wood coffee stirrers, and embellished tags—and, of course, a few words of your own.

Creating the Project

1. Tear the top edges of two consecutive pages to create a pocket.

2. Color the surface of the pocket and portions of the facing page. Stamp a design in a complementary-colored ink over the surfaces.

3. Glue the pocket to two or more backing pages for stability.

4. Punch holes along the side of the pocket to add eyelets and rings.

5. Punch holes along the edge of the backing page to add eyelets and a folded strip of decorative paper.

6. Insert colored and stamped shipping tags—decorated with messages or interesting details—into the pockets.

7. Glue the facing page to a backing page.

8. Embellish a few coffee stirrers with stamped strips of random verse. Attach the coffee stirrers to the facing page and backing page with eyelets.

Laurie Goodson

119

BUTTERFLY KISSES

*A*n altered book is a collaborative work between you—the artist—and the author of the book you are altering. You can directly embellish the pages of the book, incorporating the original text and illustrations into your design. Or you can remove the book's existing pages and attach new pages of your own. To make this transparent butterfly page, one of the actual book pages is replaced with a sheet of acetate, which is attached between two narrow strips of torn pages.

Laurie Goodson

Creating the Project

1. Tear two consecutive pages, leaving two roughly 1-inch tabs extending out of the fold of the book.

2. Glue a sheet of acetate—the same size as the book page—between the tabs. Freehand cut a decorative edge on the page.

3. Color the full page before and the full page following the acetate page.

4. Glue each of the colored pages to a backing page.

5. Punch three holes in the upper edge of the right-hand page and attach a folded decorative paper with eyelets.

6. Punch several butterfly wings from colored and patterned papers—choose a color that will complement the color of the pages. Attach the punched shapes randomly to the pages. Glue the body only of the butterflies to the page, leaving the wings free to flutter.

7. Decorate several realistic butterfly stickers with glitter paint or glue. Apply these butterflies to the acetate page.

8. Add a title to your acetate page by stamping or writing onto a transparent adhesive label.

CHESS PAGES

*T*hese pages combine techniques and materials to add depth and dimension to the design. Holes punched in consecutive pages mark the spot for a miniature compass. Silky decorative ribbons are woven in horizontal strips through careful slits in two glued pages—to create a decorative and textural effect, front and back.

Creating the Project

1. Stipple or stamp both pages with ochre and dark brown inks.

2. Make a hole in the upper right-hand corner of the right-hand page with a 1-inch circle punch. Working with this first hole as a guide, punch through the next 50 pages or so—to make a hole deep enough to accommodate the height of your miniature compass. (Test the fit as you work to determine when you have punched through enough pages.) Glue the compass to the last page.

3. Glue each page of the spread to a backing page to give the pages more body (the paper in old books can be brittle and may tear or crumble easily).

Kim Smith

4. Place a cutting mat behind the right-hand page. With a craft knife, cut an even number of vertical lines (8 here), leaving an uncut frame at the bottom and top of the page. You can use the lines of text themselves as cutting guides.

5. Starting at the top of the page, weave a length of ribbon horizontally in and out of the cut vertical lines. Start each ribbon at the spine of the book. Let the ribbons extend about ½ inch off the edge of the page so that they hang like bookmarks. Continue weaving until you fill the page.

6. Glue both ends of each ribbon to the surface of the page. Attach a vertical ribbon close to the spine on the front and back of the page to cover the raw edges. Cut the overhanging lengths to make forked ends.

7. Attach punched shapes and other embellishments to the facing page to support your theme.

FRENCH BULLETIN BOARD PAGE

*R*emove the book's existing pages and attach new pages of your own—or work directly on the pages, incorporating the original text and illustrations into your composition—or transform them into a colorful background pattern, as this artist did here.

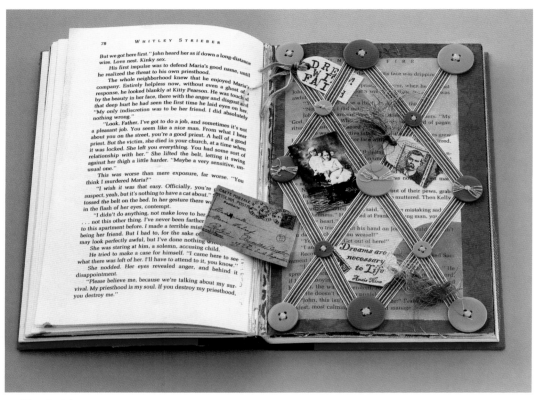

Kim Smith

TIP

If the book does not lie flat when closed, you may need to remove about 10 or more book pages to compensate for the height of the buttons.

Creating the Project

1. Apply a mask on the page over the text. Mask the border, too, aligning the edge with the edge of the text mask.

2. Place a cutting mat under the page and lightly cut several random shapes in the text mask—do not to cut through the book's pages or border.

3. Carefully remove a center section of the text mask and color the paper with a direct-to-paper technique. Replace the mask and repeat the process to color the other sections.

4. Remove the border mask and add a frame of dark color. Roller stamp a design or texture. Remove the rest of the masks.

5. Cut two lengths of ribbon to form a large X diagonally across the text. Glue the ribbons at both ends and at their intersection.

6. Position four shorter ribbons parallel to the legs of the central X, so that there is one on each side of each leg. Glue all the ribbons at ends and intersections. Apply a threaded adhesive button at each intersection.

7. Punch out tag shapes and stamp with images that support your theme. Add yarn or ribbon to make pulls for the tags. Slide the tags, small photographs, and other "memorabilia" under the X's.

WINNING HAND POP-UP PAGE

*T*he centerpiece of this book—which has "games" as its theme—is an eye-popping pop-up card game page. The pop-ups are made with blank playing cards, which are stamped with a near-royal flush using River City Stamps.

Creating the Project

1. Stipple the background on both pages with dye-based ink. Stipple a sheet of large-diamond-shaped stickers and stamp with a texture stamp. (Or cut diamond shapes from cardstock.)

2. Apply the diamonds to form a harlequin pattern across both pages. Start halfway down the left-hand page, butting the point of a diamond with the fold. Work from the center to the outer edge of the page and place the diamonds across both pages, aligning them at their points. (Diamond shapes of text blocks will show between the diamond stickers.)

Kim Smith

3. Stamp blank playing cards to create the face cards and the 10 of diamonds. Stipple the cards to "age" them slightly. To create the pop-up, position two cards on either side of the center card. The center card should overlap the front edges of the two adjacent cards by about ¼ inch. Glue the cards together. Position and glue two more cards to the outer cards, again overlapping the edges by ¼ inch.

4. Create the pop-up stand by cutting a strip of cardstock that is the same length as the pop-up and about half the height. Fold the edge of the cardstock lengthwise to make a ½-inch tab on the base. Fold the cardstock in half widthwise and cut a ½-inch-wide V in the center fold of the base. Attach the tab to the back of the pop-up, aligning the center folds of both pieces.

5. Fold the pop-up in half widthwise. With the top edge facing the bottom of the book, insert the bottom edge into the spine at a 45-degree angle. Holding the pop-up at that angle, glue one-half of the base to each page. Close the book to seat the pop-up in the fold.

6. Punch out diamond, spade, heart, and club shapes. Arrange them decoratively across the pages. "Antique" a few mini playing cards by sanding the edges and stippling with ochre and dark brown ink. Glue the cards separately or in fan shapes and add letter stickers to title your page.

SOURCE GUIDE

For products used, contact the companies for a retail store near you. If you do not have a store nearby, most of the products may be purchased from the Great American Stamp Store (203-221-1229).

SUPPLIERS

A MUSE ART STAMPS
877-783-4882
www.amuseartstamps.com

AMERICAN TAG
800-223-3956
www.americantag.net

ARTISTIC WIRE
www.artisticwire.com

C-THRU RULER
860-243-0303
www.cthruruler.com

ECSTASY CRAFTS
888-288-7131
www.ecstasycrafts.com

EK SUCCESS
www.eksuccess.com

EMAGINATION CRAFTS
www.emaginationcrafts.com

FISKARS
www.fiskars.com

HERO ARTS
800-822-4376
www.heroarts.com

IMPRESS
www.impressrubberstamps.com

JAPANESE PAPER PLACE
www.japanesepaperplace.com

JUDIKINS
www.judikins.com

LAKE CITY CRAFTS
www.lakecitycrafts.com

LASTING IMPRESSIONS
801-298-1979
www.lastingimpressions.com

MAGENTA
450-922-5253
www.magentastyle.com

MARVY UCHIDA
www.uchidaofamerica.com

McGILL, INC.
www.mcgillinc.com

MEMORY BOX
888-723-1484
www.memorybox.com

MOOTE POINTS
www.mootepoints.com

MRS. GROSSMAN'S
www.mrsgrossmans.com

MY SENTIMENTS EXACTLY
719-260-6001
www.sentiments.com

PENNY BLACK
510-849-1883
www.pennyblackinc.com

PETITE MOTIFS
425-985-5261
www.petitemotifs.com

PRINTWORKS
800-854-6558

RIVER CITY RUBBER WORKS
316-529-8656
www.rivercityrubberworks.com

RUBBER STAMPEDE
800-632-8386
www.rubberstampede.com

SAKURA
www.gellyroll.com

SAVVY STAMPS
360-833-4555
www.savvystamps.com

RUBBER STAMPING PROJECT MATERIALS

PAGE 14 TOP
Ribbon/Brads (Creative Impressions)
Punch (Marvy Uchida)
Stamp (EK Success)
Paper (Lasting Impressions)

PAGE 15 ALL CARDS
Stamps/Paper (Memory Box)

PAGE 16 ALL CARDS
Stamps/Paper (Savvy)

PAGE 17 BOTH CARDS
Stamps/Buttons (Hero Arts)

PAGE 18 TOP
Stamps (Savvy)
Tag (Making Memories)

PAGE 18 BOTTOM
Stamps (A Muse Art Stamps)

PAGE 19 TOP RIGHT, BOTTOM RIGHT
Stamps (Savvy, My Sentiments Exactly)

PAGE 19 MIDDLE
Stamps (Savvy)
Pocket Template (River City Rubber Works)
Tags (American Tag)

PAGE 20 TOP
Stamps (Penny Black)
Glitter Glue (Ranger Ink)

PAGE 20 BOTTOM
Stamps (Memory Box)

PAGE 21 ALL CARDS
Stamps (Impress, Savvy)

PAGE 22 BOTH CARDS
Stamps/Paper (Printworks)
Embossing Powder (JudiKins)

PAGE 23 TOP
Stamps (Printworks)
Embossing Powder (JudiKins)

PAGE 23 BOTTOM (BOTH CARDS)
Stamps/Paper (Magenta)

PAGES 24, 25 ALL CARDS
Stamps/Paper (My Sentiments Exactly)
Photo Corners (Kolo)

PAGE 26 BOTH CARDS
Stamp (Magenta, Savvy)
Punch (Marvy Uchida)

PAGE 27 TOP
Stamps (Magenta, Stacey Stamps)

PAGE 27 BOTTOM
Stamp (My Sentiments Exactly)
Photo Corners (Kolo)

PAGES 28, 29
Stamps & Frame Kit (Magenta)

PAGE 30
Stamps (Rubber Stampede)

PAGE 31 (BOTH CARDS)
Stamps (Rubber Stampede, Savvy)

PUNCH ART PROJECT MATERIALS

PAGE 34
Punches (EK Success, Marvy Uchida)

PAGE 35 TOP
Punch (EK Success)

PAGE 35 BOTTOM
Punch (Emagination Crafts, Marvy Uchida)
Stamp (Magenta)

PAGE 36
Embossing System (Fiskars)
Punches (Marvy Uchida)
Template (Lasting Impressions)

PAGE 37 TOP
Punch (Marvy Uchida)
Stamp (Savvy)
Wire (Artistic Wire)

PAGE 37 BOTTOM
Punches (Emagination Crafts, McGill)
Trimmer (Fiskars)
Texture Plate (Fiskars)

PAGES 38, 39
Punches (Marvy Uchida, EK Success, Fiskars)

PAGE 40 TOP
Stamps (A Muse Art Stamps)
Punches (Fiskars)

PAGE 40 BOTTOM
Punches (Marvy Uchida, EK Success)
Stickers (EK Success)

PAGE 41 TOP
Punch (Emagination Crafts)

PAGE 41 BOTTOM
Stamps, Flowers (Savvy)
Paper (Memory Box)
Punch (Marvy Uchida)

PAGE 42 TOP
Stamp (Hero Arts)
Punch (Marvy Uchida, EK Success)

PAGE 42 BOTTOM
Punches (EK Success, Marvy Uchida)
Ribbon (Mary Arts)

PAGE 43 TOP
Punch (EK Success)
Tag (American Tag)
Paper (Savvy)

PAGE 43 BOTTOM
Punches (EK Success)

PAGES 44, 45 ALL CARDS
Punches (Marvy Uchida, EK Success, Emaginations)
Wire (Artistic Wire)
Stamps (My Sentiments Exactly)

PAGE 46
Texture Plates (Fiskars)
Embossing System (Fiskars)
Punch (EK Success)

PAGE 47 TOP RIGHT
Texture Plates (Fiskars)
Embossing System (Fiskars)
Punch (EK Success)

PAGE 47 MIDDLE
Punches (Marvy Uchida, EK Success)
Glaze Pens (Sakura)

PAGE 47 BOTTOM LEFT
Punches (Marvy Uchida)
Embossing System (Fiskars)
Paper (Fiskars)

PAGE 48 TOP
Punches (Marvy Uchida, EK Success)

PAGE 48 BOTTOM
Punches (Emagination Crafts, McGill)

PAGE 49 TOP
Punch (McGill, Marvy Uchida)
Tag (American Tag)

PAGE 49 BOTTOM
Stamps (A Muse Art Stamps)
Punches (Fiskars)

PAGES 50, 51 ALL PROJECTS
Punches (Marvy Uchida, EK Success, McGill Chalk)
Adornments (Creative Impressions)
Paper (C-Thru Ruler, Printworks)

STICKER ART PROJECT MATERIALS

PAGE 54 BOTH CARDS
Stickers (Gingko Leaves)
Paper (Crinkle Paper, Vellum, Etal Paper)

PAGE 55 LEFT
Stickers (Textured Tags, Vellum Metallic Gingko, Scrapbook Blocks, Full Sheet Noisette)
Paper (Ribbed Paper)
Other Supplies (Funky Fibers)

TEMPLATES

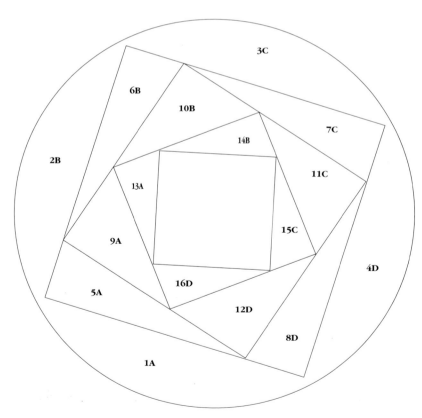

IRIS FOLDING TEMPLATE PG. 68

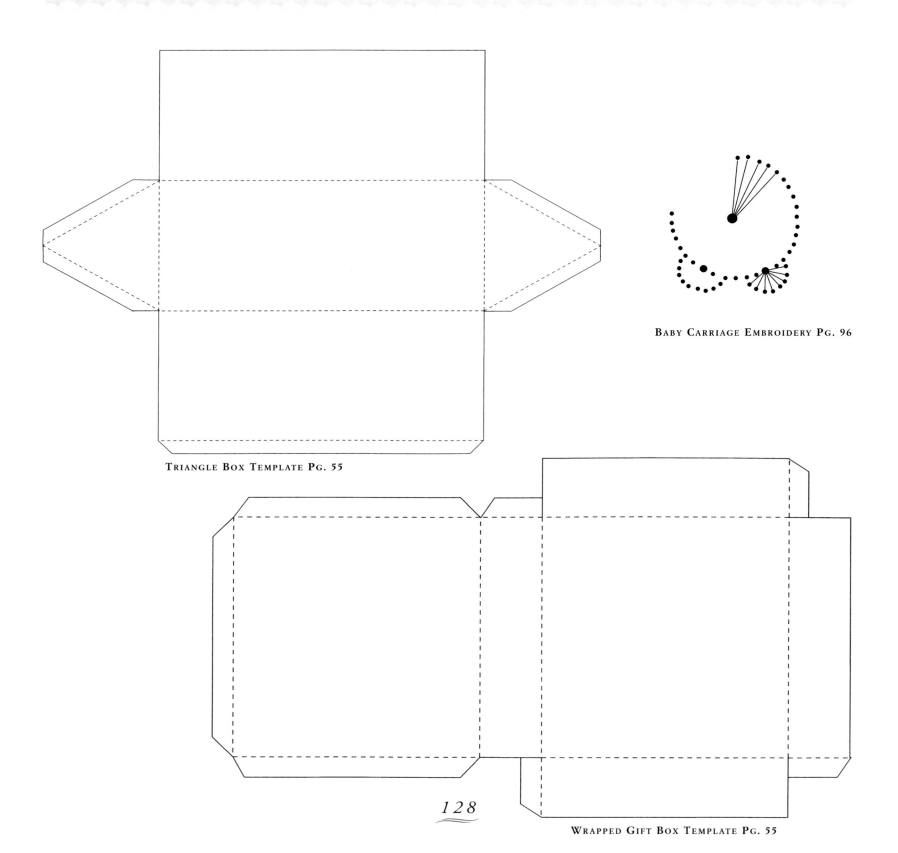

BABY CARRIAGE EMBROIDERY PG. 96

TRIANGLE BOX TEMPLATE PG. 55

WRAPPED GIFT BOX TEMPLATE PG. 55

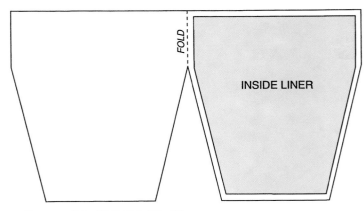

INSIDE LINER

FOLD

FLOWER POT PATTERN PG. 56

BIB TEMPLATE PG. 97

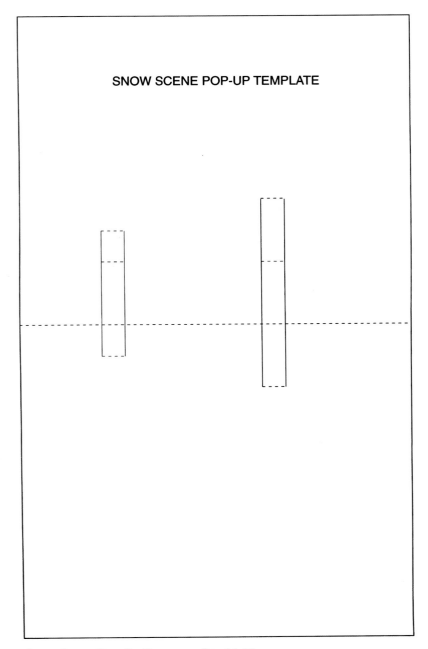

SNOW SCENE POP-UP TEMPLATE

SNOW SCENE POP-UP TEMPLATE PG. 64-65

TUMBLING BLOCKS QUILT TEMPLATE PG. 107

ILLUSTRATED GLOSSARY

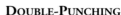

ACCORDION BOOKS

Accordion books are small folded booklets often created from one sheet of paper. *See page 78.*

ALTERED BOOKS

Altered books are hardcover books that are turned into individual works of art by tearing, cutting, or folding the pages, and adding ink, stickers, stamps, punches, mementos, fabric—just about anything. *See page 119.*

BARGELLO

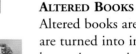
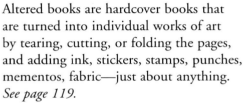

Bargello is a seventeenth-century Florentine style of needlepoint, characterized by a geometric pattern and zigzag "flame" stitch, that quilters and paper crafters have adapted to embellish their projects. *See page 87.*

COLLAGE

Collage is a collection of artfully arranged images, papers, or other materials pasted together on a page or paper-covered object. *See page 84 (top).*

DIRECT-TO-PAPER INKING TECHNIQUE

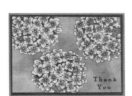

Direct-to-paper is a technique of applying ink onto paper with an ink pad, Cat's Eyes®, dauber, or other inking tool. Pigment inks work best because they can be blended before they dry. *See page 31 (top).*

DOUBLE-PUNCHING

Double-punching is the technique of punching a single image from two different pieces of paper, then cutting out part of one image and attaching it to the other. *See page 47 (middle).*

EMBOSSING, DRY

Dry-embossing is the technique of raising an image on paper using a brass (or other metal) stencil and rubbing the surface with a stylus. *See page 46.*

EMBOSSING, INK

Ink-embossing is the process of raising an inked image by applying a special powder which, when heated, rises up and becomes permanent. *See page 27 (bottom).*

IRIS FOLDING

Iris folding involves arranging folded strips of paper in a spiral pattern around a central opening, similar to the iris of the eye or the lens of a camera. *See page 69 (top).*

MASKING

Masking is the process of covering an image or the area around the image with fresh paper so that a second image can be made. Removing the mask reveals the second image in the background. *See page 14 (top).*

MOSAIC

Mosaic is basically the same for the paper crafter as for the tile artist. Photos (or paper) are cut into small shapes and placed on a page separated by a uniform space or line. *See page 89.*

ORIGAMI

Origami is the Japanese art of folding small squares of paper into representational shapes. *See page 72.*

PAPER-FOLDING

Paper-folding is the art of creating shapes from paper by folding and assembling papers into attractive designs to produce frames, borders, and embellishments for a scrapbook page or card. *See page 76.*

PAPER LAYERING

Paper layering can mean cutting out parts of a design to allow a different colored paper to show through; placing light paper, like vellum, over an image to screen or soften the image or color underneath *(see page 44)*; or framing an image by placing multiple papers behind *(see page 51, middle).*

PAPER PIERCING

Paper piercing is a technique used to accent designs by pricking small holes in the paper with a needle or awl. It works well with parchment paper or vellum, which allow the backing paper to show through, or on cardstock, which adds texture to the finished project.
See page 98 (top).

PAPER QUILTING

Quilt designs, cut from various shaped patterns, can be adapted to create stunning borders, frames, or even the central motif on a page. *See page 107.*

PAPER WEAVING

Paper weaving involves interlacing strips of paper of contrasting or complementary colors, textures, or patterns to create the illusion of woven fabrics. *See page 97.*

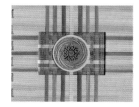

POP-UP CONSTRUCTION

Pop-up construction is the art of cutting, folding, and mounting an image so that when you open a card the design literally pops up from the inside. *See page 65.*

QUILLING

Quilling is a simple decorative technique accomplished by rolling thin strips of paper around a slotted or needle tool into various shapes and then arranging and combining the shapes to embellish your design. *See page 109.*

SPIRELLI

Spirelli, or string art, is the art of creating linear geometric patterns of different colored threads to embellish a design. *See page 102.*